MILL'S
ON LIBERTY

Critical Essays on the Classics
General Editor: Steven M. Cahn

This new series is designed to introduce college students to major works of philosophical and political theory through the best critical essays on those works. The distinguished editors of each collection have selected essays for their scholarly excellence and their accessibility to students. Each collection is meant to serve as a companion to the work itself, providing a gateway into a deeper understanding of the text.

Forthcoming in the series:

MILL'S
ON LIBERTY

Critical Essays

EDITED BY
GERALD DWORKIN

ROWMAN & LITTLEFIELD PUBLISHERS, INC.
Lanham • New York • Boulder • Oxford

ROWMAN & LITTLEFIELD PUBLISHERS, INC.

Published in the United States of America
by Rowman & Littlefield Publishers, Inc.
4720 Boston Way, Lanham, Maryland 20706

12 Hid's Copse Road
Cummor Hill, Oxford OX2 9JJ, England

British Library Cataloguing in Publication Information Available

Library of Congress Cataloging-in-Publication Data

Mill's On Liberty: critical essays / edited by Gerald Dworkin.
    p. cm. — (Critical essays on the classics)
    Includes bibliographical references and index.
    ISBN 0-8476-8488-1 (cloth : alk. paper). — ISBN 0-8476-8489-X
(pbk. : alk. paper)
    1. Mill, John Stuart, 1806–1873. On liberty. 2. Liberty.
I. Dworkin, Gerald. II. Series.
JC585.M75M55 1997
323.44—dc21   97-1792
                                    CIP

ISBN 0-8476-8488-1 (cloth : alk. paper)
ISBN 0-8476-8489-X (pbk. : alk. paper)

Printed in the United States of America

♾™ The paper used in this publication meets the minimum requirements of American National Standard for Information Sciences—Permanence of Paper for Printed Library Materials, ANSI Z39.48–1984.

For Lisa and Julie

Contents

Preface

It is rather surprising that a nineteenth-century English philosopher, who published his main work on the topic of liberty in 1859, should still be so influential in many of the most important contemporary American debates about the role of the state in limiting liberty. Whether the issue is the censorship of pornography, hate speech on college campuses, the legalization of drugs, gay rights, the equality of women, or whether motorcyclists should have to wear helmets, the views of John Stuart Mill are frequently cited.

Even those who take positions opposed to Mill's feel compelled to confront his views. Feminists who wish to limit in some way the distribution of pornography, defenders of some kinds of limited paternalism (seat-belt laws, laws requiring hunters to wear bright vests), and campus administrators who want to prohibit students from taunting others with racial epithets often try to show how Mill's arguments on these matters are defective or more limited in their scope than he thought.

Consider, for example, a recent Kentucky Supreme Court decision on a statute against homosexual sex, which specified that "consent of the other person shall not be a defense." The majority opinion overturned the statute stating that "where one seeks happiness in private, removed from others (indeed unknown to others, absent prying), and where the conduct is not relational to the rights of another, state interference is per se overweening, arbitrary, and unconstitutional." The dissenters correctly recognize that

> this view represents the essence of the philosophy of John Stuart Mill in his essay on Liberty. . . . While the philosophy of John Stuart Mill as adopted by this Court . . . exalts individuality in the extreme, it has, nevertheless, a superficial appeal. . . . Unfortunately for the purposes of the majority, the philosophy of Mill . . . if logically applied, would necessarily result in the eradi-

cation of numerous other criminal statutes. For example, if majoritarian morality is without a role in the formulation of criminal law and the only standard is harm to another, all laws proscribing the possession and use of dangerous or narcotic drugs would fail.[1]

So the battle is joined; where would the consistent application of Mill's views lead and is that a place we would not wish to go?

Why is it that Mill's views continue to have such influence? The shortest answer is: he was right. But this cannot be the whole story for he was surely (sometimes) wrong, and even if he were wholly right, why do other philosophers who have similar views, such as von Humboldt, not have similar influence?

I

Part of the story reflects the nature of a large portion of current normative controversy. Much contemporary debate concerns the issue of the legitimate boundaries of state power, i.e., the use of legal coercion. Matters could have been different; indeed, at different times in our history, they were. In the early part of the twentieth century much controversy was focused on the nature of large corporations and their exercise of authority and power. In the 1950s there was much discussion of the "lonely individual" and the threat of conformity imposed by social sanctions—a topic also of great interest for Mill. Today, for better or worse, the central political issues tend to be whether the role of government should be expanded or restricted. Hence, the importance of a philosopher whose work focuses on this question.

The second important consideration is that we are an increasingly heterogeneous society. Many different religions, cultures, classes, and normative systems compete for public attention and favor. This raises questions about the extent to which different viewpoints should be allowed to be heard. When there are intense differences in moral outlooks, what attitudes should be taken toward those with whom one disagrees? Can the state take sides in these debates or must it remain neutral about competing viewpoints? Is tolerance a virtue or an indication of lack of conviction?

These are exactly the questions that Mill grappled with more than a hundred years ago.

Other philosophers wrote about these issues and expressed views quite similar to those Mill expressed. Why were their views not as influential? Here we have to look to the philosophical framework that Mill used to argue for his views. Mill was a Utilitarian. Utilitarianism is a familiar framework even to those who are not philosophically sophisticated. Whenever we try to decide what to do by tallying up the benefits of a proposed course of action and weighing them against the costs we are engaged in a kind of utilitarian reasoning. Utilitarianism is a secular framework; there is no appeal to a faith that may be unfamiliar or abhorrent to some. Utilitarianism is a doctrine that is quite consistent with the scientific world outlook. Indeed it turns normative questions into empirical questions about the consequences of our actions. These questions may be very difficult to answer but, in principle, they are open to scientific reasoning and judgment. For all these reasons the kind of reasoning used by Mill is both familiar and fits the current paradigms of rationality.

In terms of the substantive conclusions Mill reaches they are again congenial to a liberal, democratic society. The state ought to be limited in its use of the coercive sanctions of the law to preventing people from harming one another. "The only purpose for which power can be rightfully exercised over any member of a civilized society against his will is to prevent harm to others."[2] The corollary is that the state ought not to be in the business of preventing people from harming themselves or making people more virtuous. It also ought not to interfere when people regard themselves as offended by the conduct of others, particularly if the offense arises at the mere thought that other people are engaged in the conduct in question.

But it is important to note that Mill did not believe in a "neutral" state. He did not think that the state ought not to care about the nature of its citizens' character.

> It would be a great misunderstanding of this doctrine, to suppose that it is one of selfish indifference, which pretends that human

beings have no business with each other's conduct in life, and that they should not concern themselves about the well-doing or well-being of one another, unless their own interest is involved. Instead of any diminution, there is need of a great increase of disinterested exertion to promote the good of others. But disinterested benevolence can find other instruments to persuade people to their good, than whips and scourges, either of the literal or of the metaphorical sort.[3]

It was only the use of coercion that Mill ruled out in such absolute terms. This is partly because he thought that such methods are ineffective in accomplishing their aims. But, just as important, he thought that the idea of coercing people to virtue made no sense.

Mill's views are the same with respect to free speech. Those who advocated false and pernicious doctrines should not be suppressed. But this did not mean that he embraced a relativism that did not distinguish between the true and the false, the sound and the unsound. False and pernicious views should be met with withering and accurate criticism. The way to combat harmful speech is with more speech, not with less. His view that when we suppress speech we assume we are infallible has been met with the seemingly devastating criticism that in suppressing false views we only assume that we are correct (although fallible). Mill's point, however, is methodological; we are only entitled to assume we are correct if our views have been exposed to the widest range of differing and critical opinions.

In terms, then, of both its substance and form, Mill's views cohere well with contemporary moral and legal opinion. *On Liberty* is a classic—a work that continues to enlighten and support our best thinking on contemporary issues of vital importance to a democratic society.

Notes

1. *Commonwealth of Kentucky v Jeffrey Wasson.*
2. J. S. Mill, *On Liberty* (London: J. W. Parker & Son, 1859), chapt. I.
3. Ibid., chapt. IV.

Acknowledgments

The editor and publisher thank the authors and publishers of the following essays for permission to reprint them in this volume.

Chapter 1, "Mill and Milquetoast" by David Lewis, originally appeared in *Australasian Journal of Philosophy* 67 (1989): 152–71.

Chapter 2, "John Stuart Mill and the Harm of Pornography" by David Dyzenhaus, originally appeared in *Ethics* 102 (April 1992): 534–51.

Chapter 3, "Mill and Pornography" by Robert Skipper, originally appeared in *Ethics* 103 (July 1993): 726–30.

Chapter 4, "Paternalism" by Gerald Dworkin, originally appeared in *The Monist* 56, no. 1 (June 1972): 64–84.

Chapter 5, "Paternalism, Utility, and Fairness" by Richard Arneson, originally appeared in *Revue Internationale de Philosophie* 170 (March 1989): 409–23.

Chapter 6, "Liberty and Harm to Others" by David Lyons, originally appeared in *Canadian Journal of Philosophy* Supplementary Volume V (1979): 1–19.

Chapter 7, "Profound Offense" by Joel Feinberg, originally appeared in *Offense to Others*, volume 2 of *The Moral Limits of the Criminal Law* (New York: Oxford University Press, 1985), 50–72.

Chapter 8, "The Doctrine of Liberty in Its Application to Morals" by James Fitzjames Stephen, originally appeared in *Liberty, Equality, Fraternity* (London, 1873), 126–42.

1

Mill and Milquetoast

David Lewis

1. Toleration

We are fortunate to live under institutions of toleration. Opinions that many of us deem false and pernicious are nevertheless held, and even imparted to others, with impunity. This is so in part because we hold legal rights to freedom of thought and freedom of expression. Not only do these legal rights exist; they enjoy widespread support. Any effort to revoke them would be widely opposed. Those whose opinions were threatened with suppression would find many allies, even among those who most deplored their opinions.

But legal rights are far from the whole story. The institutions of toleration are in large part informal, a matter not of law but of custom, habits of conduct and thought. Even when the law lets us do as we like, many of us do not like to do anything that would make people suffer for the opinions they hold, or hinder their expression of their opinions. We may choose our friends and our casual acquaintances as we please, and we are certainly free to shun those whose opinions we find objectionable; but many of us exercise this freedom half-heartedly, or with a bad conscience, or not at all. An editor or a bookseller has plenty of discretion to assist in the spreading of some opinions and not others, and might weigh many different considerations in deciding what to publish or what to sell; but might very well think it wrong to give any weight at all to whether an author's opinions are true or false, beneficial or dangerous.

1

Not only do customs of toleration complement legal rights; to some extent, the customs may even substitute for the rights. Doubtless it is a good idea to entrench toleration by writing it into the constitution and the statutes. But the measure of toleration need not be legalistic. The real test is: what can you get away with? What opinions can you express without fear of reprisal? To what extent can you reach your audience, if it wants to be reached? What can you read or hear without fear of reprisal? If the samizdat circulate freely, and you needn't be a hero to write or produce or read them, that is not yet good enough. But it is very much more than nothing. A country where banned books become contraband best-sellers is worse off than a country where books cannot be banned at all; but their difference is not great when we compare them both with a country where banned books really do disappear.

Toleration need not be everywhere to be effective. An atheist is not welcome everywhere—who is?—and if he cannot find toleration in the place he most wants to be, to that extent he suffers for his opinions. But if there are many and varied places where an atheist is perfectly welcome, then he doesn't suffer much. Likewise, it is essential that there should be some magazines where atheism may be published; it matters little that there are many others where it may not. Even a handful of urban and rural bohemias can go a long way toward making toleration available to those who have need of it. So if an intolerant majority do not bestir themselves to clean up the bohemias, then even they are participating in the institutions of toleration.

2. Mill's Project

That is what toleration is. Now, what is it good for? In his *On Liberty*, Mill undertakes to give it a utilitarian defence.[1] That is, he undertakes to show that its expected benefits outweigh its expected costs. But he is no simplistic Benthamite: 'I regard utility as the ultimate appeal on all ethical questions; but it must be utility in the largest sense, grounded on the permanent interests of man as a progressive being.' (p. 14) So whatever commitments

Mill may incur elsewhere, here we needn't worry whether matters of human flourishing somehow translate into a common currency of pleasure and pain.

All the same, we had better not take utility in *too* large a sense. 'I forego any advantage from the idea of an abstract right as a thing independent of utility.' (p.14) So it will not do to claim that the infringement of such 'abstract' rights is itself one cost to be weighed in the balance as a component of 'utility', whether with infinite weight (as a 'side constraint') or just as one consideration among others.

There seems to be another rule to Mill's game, unannounced but manifest in his practice. Let us make it explicit. It is the rule of *neutralism.* Suppose we have a dispute, say between believers and atheists, and suppose the believers want to suppress what they take to be the false and dangerous opinions of the atheists. Some utilitarian atheist might defend toleration thus: in the first place there is no God, therefore no harm can come of holding beliefs offensive to God. Nor can the spread of atheism do harm in any other way. Therefore suppressing atheism has no benefits to match its costs. Therefore toleration would be better. This defence is utilitarian, sure enough; but unMillian. The Millian defender of toleration makes his case without taking sides in the dispute. Of course he may argue from factual premises—no utilitarian could go far without them!—but not from factual premises that are part of the very dispute between the suppressors and the suppressed. It is Mill's ambition to defend toleration even when questions remain disputed, therefore it will not do to require some settlement of the dispute before the case for toleration can be completed.

The neutralism of Mill's practice goes further. Some utilitarian might say to the believers that according to their opinion toleration maximises utility because God is offended more by the cruelty of inquisitors than by the impudence of atheists; and might argue to the atheists that according to their opinion toleration maximises utility because there is no God to be offended. This playing both sides of the street is a valid argument by separation of cases: *A* or *B*, if *A* then toleration maximises utility, if *B* then toleration maximises utility, therefore toleration maximises utility in either case. But however valid it may be, this too is unMillian. In a Millian defence of toleration, not only must the factual premises be common ground between the two sides; also a uniform and non-disjunctive argument must be addressed to both. The Millian invites both sides to assent to a single, common list of the benefits of toleration and costs of suppression. This common list is supposed to have decisive weight in favour of toleration. One or the other side may have in mind some further costs and benefits that obtain according to its own disputed opinions, perhaps including some that count in favour of suppression; but if so, these considerations are supposed to be outweighed by the considerations on the neutral common list.

Why do I ascribe a rule of neutralism to Mill? Only because I never see him violate it. Not because he states and defends it—he does not. And not because it is in any way essential to his project of defending toleration by appeal to utility. On the contrary. To decide whether he himself should think that toleration maximises utility, Mill must sum up all the relevant costs and benefits according to his own opinions. To persuade me that toleration maximises utility, he must sum them up according to my opinions (perhaps my original opinions, or perhaps my new opinions after he is done persuading me). It is irrelevant whether the opinions are disputed or undisputed. But Mill is not doing his private sums, nor is *On Liberty* addressed to some one person in particular. It is meant to persuade an audience with varied opinions. It's hard to play both sides of the street when you're writing for both sides at once! Better for Mill if he can address the whole of his case to the whole of his audience. He can do so, if a neutral common list suffices to outweigh whatever other disputed costs and benefits there may be. Hence the rule of neutralism. It makes no sense as a constraint on utilitarian argument *per se*, but plenty of sense as part of Mill's strategy of persuasion.

3. Self- and Other-Regarding

The main principle of *On Liberty*, second only to the ultimate appeal to utility in the largest sense, is that 'the sole end for which mankind are warranted . . . in interfering with the liberty of action of any of their number is self-protection.' (p.13) It is notoriously difficult to get clear about the requisite line between self- and other-regarding action. But it is worth a digression to see why the principle and the difficulty need not concern us here.

First, and decisively, because the protection of self-regarding conduct is in any case derived from the ultimate appeal to utility. It has no force of its own to justify toleration if the direct appeal to utility fails.

Second, in addition, because if an opinion is not held secretly, but is expressed in a way that might persuade others, that *is* other-regarding: both because of the effect that the opinion may have on the life of the convert and because of what the convert might do, premised on that opinion, which might affect third parties.

Mill is confusing on this point. 'The liberty of expressing and publishing opinions may seem to fall under a different principle, since it belongs to that part of the conduct of an individual which concerns other people; but, being almost of as much importance as the liberty of thought itself and resting in great part on the same reasons, is practically inseparable from it.' (p.16) What kind of argument is this? Other-regarding conduct is not in general protected by reason of inseparability from private thought, as will be plain if someone's religion demands human sacrifice.

4. Mill's Tally

I do not believe that a utilitarian defence of toleration, constrained by Mill's rule of neutralism, has any hope of success. I make no fundamental objection to broadly utilitarian reasoning, at least in such matters as this. It's just that I think the balance of costs and benefits will too easily turn out the wrong way. When we tally up the benefits of toleration that can be adduced in a neutral and uniform way, they will just not be weighty enough. They will fall sadly short of matching the benefits of suppression, calculated according to the opinions of the would-be suppressors.

I begin the tally with the items Mill himself lists.

Risk of error. True and beneficial opinion might be suppressed in the mistaken belief that it is false and harmful.

Mill says just 'true' and 'false'; the utilitarian argument requires that we say 'beneficial' and 'harmful'; there's no guarantee that these coincide, but for simplicity let's suppose they do.

Mixture. Truth and error may be found combined in one package deal, so that there's no way of suppressing the error without suppressing truth as well.

Dead dogma (reasons). Unless received opinion 'is suffered to be, and actually is, vigorously and earnestly contested, it will . . . be held in the manner of a prejudice, with little comprehension of its rational grounds.' (p.64)

Dead dogma (meaning). Further, 'the meaning of the doctrine itself will be in danger of being lost or enfeebled, and deprived of its vital effect on the character and conduct . . . cumbering the ground and preventing the growth of any real and heartfelt conviction from reason or personal experience.' (p.64)

Mill counts deadness of dogma as a harm only in case received opinion is true. But perhaps he should also think it worse, from the standpoint of human flourishing, that error should be held as dead dogma rather than in a real and heartfelt and reasoned way.

Mill's guess about what will happen if received opinion is vigorously contested seems remarkably optimistic. Will there be debate at all, and not just warfare? If there is debate, will it help the debaters think through their positions, or will they rather throw up a cloud of sophistries? If they think things through, will they discover unappreciated reasons or bedrock disagreement?

5. The Tally Extended

Mill's list so far seems too short. Why not borrow from the next chapter of *On Liberty* also? Then we could add—

Individuality. If diversity is of value, and thinking for oneself, and thoughtful choice, why aren't these things of some value even when people think up, and thoughtfully choose among, diverse errors?

Building character. The more chances you get to think and choose, the better you get at it; and being good at thinking and choosing is one big part of human flourishing. Freedom as a social condition offers exercises which conduce to freedom as a trait of character. Practice makes perfect.

This too seems more a piece of armchair psychology than a firm empirical result. Travelers' tales suggest that the hard school of the east sometimes does better than the free and easy west at building just such character as Mill rightly values. If we like guessing, we might guess that when it comes to building character, freedom and competent repression both take second place—what does best is repression bungled, with gratuitous stupidity and cruelty. That speculation seems at least as likely as Mill's—but responsible utilitarian calculation should put little faith in either one.

We noted that truth and error might be found combined in a package deal. Then if we suppress the error, we lose truth as well. But the same thing can happen even if the error we suppress is unmixed with truth.

Transformation. Future thinkers may turn our present errors into truth not just by filtering out the false parts but in more complicated ways. They may find us standing on our heads, and turn us on our feet. They may attend to old questions and give them new answers. They may borrow old ideas and transplant them into new and better settings. They may put the old errors to use in metaphors and analogies. If we suppress errors that might have been the germ of better things to come, we block progress. Does progress conduce to utility?—We may hope so, at least if it is 'utility in the largest sense, grounded on the permanent interests of man as a progressive being'.

Mill's lists of harms and benefits feature the high-faluting, interesting, speculative ones. He omits the obvious.

The insult of paternalism. If I paternalise over you, and in particular if I prevent you from being exposed to some seductive heresy, my action is manifestly premised on doubt of your competence, and on confidence in my own. You are likely to take offence both at my low opinion of you and at my pretension of superiority. No less so, if you acknowledge that I am indeed more competent than you are to govern your life. Bad enough it should be true! Do I have to rub it in?

(This is a different thing from the alleged insult of denying that you have rights. For (1) no similar insult is given when Bentham tells you that natural rights are nonsense upon stilts, yet he denies that you have rights more clearly than any paternalist does; (2) the insult may still be there even if you too are of Bentham's opinion; or (3) if you think that you once had rights but have freely given them away to me.)

More obviously still, there are—

The secret police. To do an effective job of suppression, it is necessary to build a system of informers and dossiers. Once in place, the means of suppression may be taken over and turned to new purposes. They might be used to advance the ambitions of a would-be tyrant—something all would agree (before it began, at least) in counting as a cost.[2]

The dungeon. If you wish to express or study proscribed opinions, and someone stops you, you will be displeased that your desires are frustrated. And if you are determined to go ahead, the only effective means of stopping you—the dungeon, the gulag, the asylum, the gallows—may prove somewhat unfelicific.

This completes our neutralist tally, our list of considerations that are meant to be accepted by all parties to disputed questions. One way or another, and even if we receive Mill's armchair psychology with all the doubt it deserves, we still have some rather weighty benefits of toleration and costs of suppression. But of course that's not enough. Mill wins his case only if the benefits of toleration outweigh the costs—and not only according to his own opinions, but according to the opinions of those he seeks to dissuade from suppressing. The cost of toleration, lest we forget, is that dangerous errors may flourish and spread.

6. The Inquisitor Reads Mill

McCloskey has written that 'many Christian liberals appear to be especially muddled, for, as Christians, they regard eternal salvation and moral living as being of tremendous importance and as being goods as valuable as freedom. Yet many of them deny the state even the abstract right to aid truth, morality, and religion and to impede error and evil, while at the same time they insist on its duty to promote the good of freedom. Their implicit value judgment is so obviously untenable that one cannot but suspect that it has not been made explicit and considered in its own right.' In the same vein, Quine: 'If someone firmly believes that eternal salvation and damnation hinge on embracing his particular religion, he would be callous indeed to sit tolerantly back and watch others go to hell.'[3] To dramatise their point, I imagine the Inquisitor: a thoughtful Christian, benevolent by his own lights, far from muddled and far from liberal. Can Mill persuade him to change his intolerant ways?

The Inquisitor, as I shall imagine him, is the very man Mill ought to be addressing. He agrees completely with Mill that the ultimate appeal is to utility in the largest sense. He claims no infallibility. Indeed his faith is infirm, and he is vividly aware that he just might be making a tragic mistake. He is satisfied—too quickly, perhaps—that Mill is an expert social psychologist, who knows whereof he speaks concerning the causes of dead dogma and the causes of excellent character. In short, he grants every item in the neutralist tally of costs and benefits.

His only complaint is that the tally is incomplete. He believes, in fact, that the included items have negligible weight compared to the omitted item. Heresy, so the Inquisitor believes, poisons the proper relationship between man and God. The heretic is imperfectly submissive, or sees God as nothing but a powerful sorcerer, or even finds some trace of fault in God's conduct. The consequence is eternal damnation. That is something infinitely worse than any evil whatever in this life; infinitely more weighty, therefore, than the whole of the neutralist tally. Further, damnation is not just a matter of pain. (Hellfire is no part of it, just an inadequate metaphor for what really happens.) Damnation is harm along exactly the dimension that Mill wanted us to bear in mind: it is the utter absence and the extreme opposite of human excellence and flourishing.

The Inquisitor also believes that heresy is contagious. The father of lies has fashioned it with all his cunning to appeal to our weaknesses. There is nothing mechanical about it—those never exposed to heretical teachings sometimes reinvent heresy for themselves, those who are exposed may withstand temptation—but still, those who are not exposed are a great deal safer than those who are.

The Inquisitor also believes that if he is ruthless enough in suppressing heresy, he may very well succeed. Not, of course, in eradicating heresy for all time; but in greatly reducing the incidence of exposure, and consequently in saving a great many souls from damnation.

Note well that the Inquisitor does not think that he could save the souls of heretics by forced conversion. He accepts the common wisdom that this cannot be done: forced conversion would be insincere, so it would be worthless in the sight of God. He knows no way to save the heretics themselves. What he could do by suppressing heresy, so he thinks, is to save many of those who are not yet heretics, but would succumb if exposed to heretical teachings.

The Inquisitor does not relish the suffering of heretics. As befits a utilitarian, he is moved by benevolence alone. He hates cruelty. But he needs the warning: 'if you hate cruelty, remember that nothing is so cruel in its consequences as the toleration of heresy.'[4]

Therefore the Inquisitor concludes, even after discounting properly for his uncertainty, that the balance of cost and benefit is overwhelmingly in favour of suppression. Mill's case for tolerating heresy is unpersuasive. In fact it is frivolous—serious matters are at stake! You might as well oppose the suppression of heresy on the ground that dungeons cost too much money.

Mill has lost his case.

This is not to say that the Inquisitor stumps utilitarianism itself. Mill was trying to bring off a *tour de force*: to abide by his self-imposed rule of neutralism, and yet win the argument against all comers. A more modest utilitarian might proceed in any of three ways.

One way for the utilitarian to deal with the Inquisitor is not to argue with him at all. You don't argue with the sharks; you just put up nets to keep them away from the beaches. Likewise the Inquisitor, or any other utilitarian with dangerously wrong opinions about how to maximise utility, is simply a danger to be fended off. You organise and fight. You see to it that he cannot succeed in his plan to do harm in order—as he thinks and you do not—to maximise utility.

A second way is to fight first and argue afterward. When you fight, you change the circumstances that afford the premises of a utilitarian argument. First you win the fight, then you win the argument. If you can make sure that the Inquisitor will fail in his effort to suppress heresy, you give him reason to stop trying. Though he thinks that successful persecution maximises utility, he will certainly agree that failed attempts are nothing but useless harm.

Finally, a modest utilitarian might dump the rule of neutralism. He might argue that, according to the Inquisitor's own opinions, there are advantages of toleration which are more weighty than those on the neutralist tally and which the Inquisitor had not appreciated. Or he might start by trying to change the Inquisitor's mind about the facts of theology, and only afterward try to demonstrate the utility of toleration. He might try to persuade the Inquisitor to replace his present theological opinions by different ones: atheism, perhaps, or a religion of sweetness and light and salvation for all. Or he might only try to persuade the Inquisitor to be more sceptical: to suspend judgement on matters of theology, or near enough that the uncertain danger of damnation no longer outweighs the more certain harms that are done when heresy is suppressed.

7. The Assumption of Infallibility

Mill does at one point seem to be doing just that—supporting toleration by supporting scepticism. If he did, he would not be observing the rule of neutralism. He would be putting forward not an addition to whatever his reader might have thought before, but rather a modification. And he would be a fine old pot calling the kettle black. Part of his own case rests on far-from-certain psychological premises.

But the appearance is deceptive.[5] Mill's point when he says that 'all silencing of discussion is an assumption of infallibility' (pp. 21–22) is not that we should hesitate to act on our opinions—for instance by silencing discussion we believe to be harmful—out of fear that our opinions may be wrong. For Mill very willingly agrees with the hypothetical objector who says that 'if we were never to act on our opinions, because those opinions may be wrong, we should leave all our interests uncared for, and all our duties unperformed . . . There is no such things as absolute certainty, but there is assurance sufficient for the purposes of human life. We may, and must, assume our opinion to be true for the guidance of our own conduct.' (pp. 23–24) Mill's real point is that if we are duly modest and do not assume ourselves infallible, we should have confidence in our opinions only when they have withstood the test of free discussion. A sceptic is like a traffic cop: he admonishes us to slow down in our believing. Whereas Mill is like the traffic cop in the tire advertisement: 'If you're not riding on Jetzon tires—slow down!' *That* cop doesn't want us to slow down—he wants us to buy Jetzon tires. Free discussion is the Jetzon tire that gives us license to speed, fallible though we be. To dare to do without Jetzon tires is to overrate your skill as a driver; to do without free discussion is to assume yourself infallible. 'Complete liberty of contradicting and disproving our opinion is the very condition which justifies us in assuming its truth for purposes of action; and on no other terms can a being with human faculties have any rational assurance of being right.' (p.24) Mill thus assures us that if we *do* meet the condition, then we *are* justified in acting on our opinions.

Our Inquisitor, if he takes Mill's word for this as he does on other matters, will not dare suppress heresy straightaway. First he must spend some time in free discussion with the heretics. Afterward, if they have not changed his mind, then he will deem himself justified in assuming the truth of his opinion for purposes of action; which he will do when he goes forward to suppress heresy, and burns his former partners in discussion at the stake.

Compare Herbert Marcuse, who advocated 'withdrawal of tolerance from regressive movements *before* they can become active; intolerance even toward thought, opinion, and word, and finally, intolerance . . . toward the self-styled conservatives, to the political Right' during the present 'emergency situation'.[6] If tolerance is withdrawn only after Marcuse has enjoyed it for many years, Mill cannot complain that Marcuse has not yet earned the right to act on his illiberal opinions.

8. Dangerous Opinions

The Inquisitor, apart from his anachronistic utilitarianism, is just an ogre out of the past. Might Mill's defence work well enough, if not against just any imaginable foe of toleration, at least against any we are likely to meet in the present day? I doubt it. To be sure, some of us nowadays are sanguine about dangerous opinions. Whatever harm opinions may do under other conditions, we think they pose no present danger in our part of the world. The neutralist tally is all the defence of toleration *we* need. But others of us think otherwise: they think that some of the people around them hold opinions that are not only false but harmful. I predict

that for many pairs of my readers—perhaps a majority of pairs—
one of the pair holds some opinion that the other would find profoundly dangerous.

It might be a religious or irreligious opinion that conduces, in
the opinion of the other, to contempt for oneself, for other people,
for the natural world, or for God.

It might be a political opinion favouring some social arrangement which, in the opinion of the other, is a trap—an arrangement which makes most people's lives degraded and miserable,
but which gives a few people both a stake in its continuation and
the power to prevent change.

It might be an opinion belittling some supposed danger which,
in the opinion of the other, requires us to take urgent measures
for our protection. It might be the opinion that we need not
worry about environmental hazards, or nuclear deterrence, or
Soviet imperialism, or AIDS, or addictive drugs.

It might be an opinion which, in the opinion of the other, is racist
or sexist and thereby fosters contempt and oppressive conduct.

It might be a moral opinion (say, about abortion) which, in the
opinion of the other, either condones and encourages wickedness or
else wrongly condemns what is innocent and sometimes beneficial.

In each of these cases, important matters are at stake. In each
case, the stakes involve a great deal of 'utility in the largest sense,
grounded on the permanent interests of man as a progressive
being.' To be sure, these cases are less extreme than that of the
Inquisitor and the heretics. We have no *infinite* outweighing.
Still, they are extreme enough. In each case, the disutility that is
feared from the dangerous opinion seems enough to outweigh all
the advantages of toleration according to the neutralist tally. And
this remains so even if we discount all around for uncertainty,
duly acknowledging that we are fallible.

In each case, therefore, if effective suppression were feasible, it
would seem frivolous for the foe of the dangerous opinion to stay
his hand because of any consideration Mill has an offer. If he does
stay his hand, it seems as if he lets geniality or custom or laziness
stand in the way of his wholehearted pursuit of maximum utility.

9. Morris

Take our contemporary, Henry M. Morris. He thinks, for one thing, that 'Evolution is the root of atheism, of communism, nazism, behaviorism, racism, economic imperialism, militarism, libertinism, anarchism, and all manner of anti-Christian systems of belief and practice.'[7] He thinks, for another thing, that in history and the social sciences, 'it is especially important . . . that the teacher gives a balanced presentation of both points of view [evolutionist and creationist] to students. Otherwise the process of education for living becomes a process of indoctrination and channelization, and the school degenerates into a hatchery of parrots.'[8] At any rate, he says both these things, and let us take him at his word. Doubtless he mainly has in mind the 'balanced treatment' versus purely evolutionist teaching. But what he says, and his argument for it, apply equally to the 'balanced treatment' versus the purely creationist teaching we might have expected him to favour. So evolution is dangerous in the extreme, yet it is not to be suppressed—it is not even to be left out of the curriculum for schoolchildren—lest we hatch parrots! ('Parrots', I take it, are the same thing as those who hold their opinions as dead dogma.) How can Morris possibly think that the harm of hatching parrots is remotely comparable to the harm done by 'balanced presentation' that spreads evolutionist ideas? How dare he give this feeble Millian reason for tolerating, and even spreading, such diabolically dangerous ideas? Surely, by his own lights, he is doing the Devil's work when he favours balance over suppression.

10. Milquetoast

Mill's defence—who needs it? Perhaps the sceptical who, when told any story about the harmful effects of dangerous opinions, will find it too uncertain to serve as a basis of action? Or perhaps the apathetic, who may believe the story but not think the harm really matters very much? No, because the sceptical and the apathetic will be equally unimpressed by Mill's own story about the harmful effects of suppression. Nor would Mill have wanted to address his argument to the sceptical or the apathetic. That is not how he wants us to be. He wants us to have our Jetzon tires exactly so that we *may* speed. He favours vigour, dedication, moral earnestness.

I suggest that Mill's defence of toleration might best be addressed to Caspar Milquetoast, that famous timid soul.[9] Doubtless he too is not the pupil Mill would have chosen, but at least he is in a position to put the lesson to use.

Milquetoast *does* have opinions about important and controversial matters. And he does care. He cares enough to raise his voice and bang the table in the privacy of his own house: asked if he wants *Russian* dressing on his salad, the answer is 'NO!' He isn't *always* timid. (p.185) But when he is out and about, his main goal is to avoid a quarrel. All else takes second place. He knows better than to talk to strangers on vital topics: asked what he thinks of the Dodgers' chances, he'd 'rather not say, if you don't mind'. (p. 162) And when his barber, razor in hand, asks how he's going to vote. Milquetoast fibs: 'Why-uh-er-I don't get a vote. I've been in prison—stir I mean—and I've lost my citizenship'. (p.183)

Milquetoast thinks, let us suppose, that it is a dangerous mistake to ignore the threat of Soviet imperialism. He would be hard put to explain why a rosy view of the evil empire is not dangerous enough to be worth suppressing. But he knows that this opinion is controversial. He knows that others think that the Soviet threat is bogus, and that the only real threat comes from our efforts to resist the bogus threat. How horrid to have to dispute these matters—as he surely would if he dared to suggest that the dangerous mistake should be suppressed. What to do?—Solution: bracket the controversial opinions. Keep them as opinions, somehow, in some compartment of one's mind, but ignore them in deciding what is to be done. In questions of suppression and toleration, in particular, appeal to uncontroversial considerations only. Conduct the discussion according to Mill's rule of neutralism. Then all hands can perhaps agree that the neutralist tally is right so far as it goes. And without the airing of disagreeable disagreement, we can go no further. Settle the question without acrimony, then, and we must settle it in favour of toleration. Those compartments of the mind that fear the dangerous consequences of the tolerated opinions should hold their tongues, lest they get us into strife.[10]

Milquetoast, of course, is an incompetent maximiser of utility. His conduct may be fortunate enough, if there turn out to be better reasons for toleration than we have yet considered. But his thought is simply shocking—he systematically declines to be guided by the whole of his system of opinions, ignoring the part that would engage him in unpleasant dispute. Nor is he at all keen to improve the quality of his thought by entering into discussion. That is why Mill should not be proud to have Milquetoast as his star pupil.

11. A Treaty of Toleration

To see how toleration can find a better utilitarian foundation, let us return to our story of the Inquisitor and the heretics. The Inquisitor thinks that the heretics hold a dangerous opinion—dangerous enough to be well worth suppressing, despite all the considerations on the neutralist tally. Because the Inquisitor thinks this, he in turn is a danger to the heretics. Not only does he menace their personal safety; also, if the heretics think that the spreading of their word will benefit all who embrace it, then they must see the Inquisitor as bringing disutility to all mankind. And the more there are of the orthodox, who think as the Inquisitor does, the worse it will be. It would be best, indeed, if none were left who might someday reinfect mankind with the old darkness. Important matters are at stake. And now let us suppose that the heretics, no less than the Inquisitor, are wholehearted pursuers of utility as they see it. (Utility in the largest sense.) In this way the heretics think that the Inquisitor, and all of the orthodox, hold a dangerous opinion—dangerous enough to be well worth suppressing, despite all the considerations on the neutralist tally.

I suppose that some such rough symmetry is a common, though not a necessary, feature of situations in which someone thinks that someone else's opinion is dangerous enough to be worth suppressing.

Devoted as both sides are to utility, and disagreeing as they do about where utility is to be found, what is there to do but fight it out? According to the Inquisitor's opinion, the best outcome will be victory: to vanquish the heretics and suppress their heresy. If this outcome is within reach, going for it is required. Not only is toleration not required by any appeal to utility; it is forbidden. Any restraint or mercy would be wrong. It would be self-indulgent neglect of 'the permanent interests of man as a progressive being', since the foremost of these interests is salvation. Suppose further that there is no hope of changing the Inquisitor's mind about the causes of salvation and damnation. Then there is no way—Millian or unMillian—to persuade him that it is a utilitarian mistake to suppress heresy. He has done his sums correctly, by his lights; we cannot fault them. Of course we can, and we should, fault his premises. They are both false and harmful. But there is no further mistake about what follows.

Likewise, *mutatis mutandis*, according to the heretics' opinion.

If one side has victory within reach, the utilitarian defence of toleration fails. But now suppose instead that the two sides are more or less equally matched. Victory is not so clearly within reach. Neither side can have it just for the asking. Resort to war means taking a gamble. One side or the other will win, and then the winners will suppress the dangerous opinions of the losers. Orthodoxy will triumph and heresy will vanish, at least for a time. Or else heresy will triumph and orthodoxy will vanish. Who can tell which it will be?

In deciding what he thinks of a state of toleration, the Inquisitor must compare it not just with one possible outcome of war but with both. Toleration means that both creeds go unsuppressed, they flourish side by side, they compete for adherents. Many are lost, but many are saved. How many?—It depends. The fear is that the heretics will not scruple to advance their cause by cunning deceit; the hope is that truth will have an inherent advantage, and will benefit from God's favour. Let us suppose that the Inquisitor takes a middling view of the prospect, not too pessimistic and not too optimistic. Then just as he finds victory vastly better than toleration, from the standpoint of salvation and therefore from the standpoint of utility, so he finds defeat vastly worse. According to the Inquisitor's opinion, the triumph of heresy would be a catastrophic loss of utility. The considerations on the neutralist tally have negligible weight, given the enormous amount of utility at stake. Even the pleasures of peace and the horrors of war have negligible weight. But the risk of defeat is far from negligible.

Likewise, *mutatis mutandis*, according to the heretics' opinion. The Inquisitor's fear of defeat might outweigh his hope of victory. It might seem to him that suppression of orthodoxy would be more of a loss than suppression of heresy would be a gain (more lasting, perhaps); or he might take a pessimistic view of the gamble of war, and think it more likely than not that the heretics would win. Or he might take a moderately optimistic view of how many souls could be won under toleration. One way or another, he might have reason to prefer mutual toleration, unsatisfactory stalemate though it be, to war. His reason is a utilitarian reason. But it rests entirely on what he takes to be the weighty benefits and harms at stake—not the lightweight benefits and harms on the neutralist tally.

It might happen for the heretics likewise that the fear of defeat outweighs the hope of victory. If both sides think defeat more likely than victory, one side must be mistaken, but even a thoughtful utilitarian might well make such a mistake. If both sides think defeat would be more of a loss than victory would be a gain, there needn't be any mistake on either side—except, of course, the underlying mistake that one or both are making all along about what conduces to utility.

Or the heretics also might hope to do well at winning souls under toleration. The orthodox and the heretics can expect alike to win the most souls, if they believe alike that truth, or the creed

God favours, will have the advantage. Their expectations are opposite, and one side or the other will be disappointed, but they can face competition with a common optimism.

It may happen, then, that each side prefers toleration to defeat more than it prefers victory to toleration, and therefore prefers toleration to the gamble of fighting it out.[11] Then we have a utilitarian basis for a treaty of toleration. Conditional toleration— toleration so long as the other side also practices toleration— would be an equilibrium. It would be the best that either side could do, if it were what the other side was doing. Toleration is everyone's second choice. The first choice—to suppress and yet be tolerated, to gain victory without risking defeat—is not available; the other side will see to that. The third choice is the gamble of war, and we have supposed that both sides find the odds not good enough. War would be another equilibrium, but a worse one in the opinions of both sides. The worst choice is unconditional unilateral toleration, which means letting the other side have their way unopposed.

In such a case, with two equilibria and a preference on both sides for one over the other—toleration over war—it is neither automatic nor impossible that both sides will find their way to the equilibrium they both prefer. They might get there formally, by bilateral negotiation and agreement.[12] They might get there by unilateral initiatives and invitations to reciprocate. They might drift there, gradually developing a tacit understanding. They might get there under the influence of non-utilitarian reasons, and only afterward find that they had reached the outcome that maximised utility by the lights of both sides. They might have been there all along, in accordance with ancient custom. In each case, I will say that they have arrived at a treaty of toleration—maybe explicit and formal, maybe tacit.

Some treaties need to be sustained by trust and honour, lest a cheater gain advantage. It is hard to see how such a treaty could work between strict utilitarians; because if a utilitarian thinks it will maximise utility if he gains the upper hand, and if he thinks he can gain the upper hand by breaking his sworn word, then that is what he must do. But if there are no opportunities for secret preparation and a surprise breakout, then unutilitarian means of commitment are not required. The utility of the treaty is incentive enough to keep it. Neither side wants to withdraw toleration, lest the other side should have nothing to lose by withdrawing its reciprocal toleration. Often enough, contractarian and utilitarian defences of social institutions are put forward as rivals. Not so this time—here we have a contract for utilitarians.

The hopes and fears of the two sides may or may not be such as to permit a treaty of toleration. If they are, toleration may or may not be forthcoming—war is still an equilibrium, it takes two to make the switch. But now a utilitarian friend of toleration has a case to make. This time, it is a case meant not for the sceptical or the apathetic, not for the dismayed irreligious bystanders, not for Milquetoast, but for the Inquisitor himself.

It is a thoroughly utilitarian case, but it is unMillian because it flouts the rule of neutralism. It plays both sides of the street. We say to the Inquisitor that a treaty of toleration affords his best hope for preventing the suppression of orthodoxy; we say to the heretics that it affords their best hope for preventing the suppression of heresy. Thereby we say to both that it affords the best hope for maximising utility, according to their very different lights. But there is no common list of benefits and costs. On the contrary, what we offer to each side as the greatest benefit of toleration is just what the other must see as its greater cost.[13]

12. Closing the Gap

While a utilitarian defence of some sort of toleration has been accomplished, or so I claim, it seems not yet to be the right sort. This grudging truce between enemies, who would be at each other's throats but for their fear of defeat, is a far cry from the institutions of toleration we know and love. Our simple story of the orthodox and the heretics differs in several ways from the real world of toleration.

Cheerful toleration. If we want to uphold a treaty of toleration, and doing our part means letting harmful error flourish, then we have to do it; but we don't have to like it. Why should we? Whereas we are proud of our institutions of toleration, and pleased to see the spectrum of diverse opinions that flourish unsuppressed. Without the ones we take to be harmful errors, the diversity would be less and we would be less well pleased. Our feelings are mixed, of course. We do not wholeheartedly welcome the errors. But we do to a significant, and bizarre, degree.

Thoughtless toleration. In the story, the defence depends on the details of the strategic balance between the two sides. Whereas in the real world, we never stop to think how the fortunes of war might go before we take for granted that toleration is better.

Tolerating the weak. In particular, we tolerate the weak. If our Inquisitor had the chance to nip heresy in the bud, long before there was any chance that the heretics might have the strength to win and suppress orthodoxy, of course he would do it. Whereas we treasure the liberty of the weak, and proclaim that the minority of one means as much to us as any other minority.

Tolerating the intolerant. There is no sense in making a treaty with someone who declares that he will not abide by it. If we tolerate harmful error as a *quid pro quo*, so that others will reciprocate by tolerating beneficial truths, why continue after they announce that they will not reciprocate? Whereas we tolerate the intolerant, no less than the tolerant. We do it; and almost everyone who cares for toleration thinks we ought to do it. After Marcuse said that the time had come to withdraw tolerance, his books were no harder to buy than they were before.

Tolerating the extra-dangerous. In the story, the utilitarian defence may depend also on the exact balance of good and harm that we expect from the several opinions that will be protected by a treaty of toleration. The more danger heresy seems to pose, the less likely our Inquisitor is to conclude that a treaty with the heretics might be advantageous. Whereas we, for the most part, favour tolerating all dangerous opinions alike, without seeking exceptions for the very most dangerous.

One difference between our simple story and the real world, of course, is that in the real world we are not all utilitarians. We may be content to mind our own business, and insist that it is not our business to protect mankind against the harm done by dangerous opinions. Or we may be devotees of the 'abstract rights' foresworn by Mill; then we may think that the rights of others constrain us not to serve utility by suppressing dangerous opinions, no matter how high the stakes. (Or they may constrain us to renounce only the harshest methods of suppression. But if only the harshest methods could succeed, we will not need any very weighty utilitarian reasons to dissuade us from trying the ineffective milder methods.)

These differences certainly work in favour of toleration—cheerful and thoughtless toleration, and toleration even of the weak, the intolerant, and the extra-dangerous. But let us not rely on them. Let us rather stay with the fiction of a population of wholehearted utilitarians, so that we may retain as much common ground with Mill as possible. Even so, I think we can close the gap between toleration as we find it in the simple story and toleration as we find it in the real world. We need not abandon the idea of a treaty of toleration. Instead, we must find the right way to extend the idea from our simple two-sided case to a complicated case, many-sided and always changing.

In the real world, there are many different factions. They differ in their opinions, they differ in their opinion about one another's opinions, and they differ in strength. As time goes by, factions wax and wane, and split and merge. The weak may suddenly gang up in a strong alliance, or an alliance may break up and leave the former allies weak. The people who comprise the factions change their minds. Circumstances also change. As the complicated situation changes, understanding of it will lag. Nobody will know very well who deplores whose opinions how much, and with how much strength to back up his deploring. In this complicated world, no less than in the simple case, some will find the opinions of others dangerous, and worthy of suppression; and some will think their own opinions beneficial, and will seek to protect them from suppression. Many would think it worthwhile to tolerate the most deplorable opinions, if they could thereby secure reciprocal toleration from others. They would welcome toleration by treaty. But how can they arrange it?

There might be a vast network of little treaties, each one repeating in miniature our story of the treaty between the orthodox and the heretics. Each faction would have protection from its treaty partners, and if it had chosen its partners well, that would give it the protection it needs. Each faction would extend toleration so far as its treaties require, and no farther. Two factions would enter into a treaty only when both thought it advantageous, given the strategic balance between them, their estimate of the fortunes of war, and their estimate of the potential for good or harm of the opinions that would be protected. The weak, who can offer no reciprocal toleration worth seeking, and the fanatically intolerant, who will not offer reciprocal toleration, would of course be left out of the network of treaties. Those whose opinions were thought to be extra-dangerous also would tend to be left out, other things being equal. A treaty would end when either side thought it no longer advantageous, or when either side thought (rightly or wrongly) that the other side was breaking it.

The trouble is plain to see. It would be enormously difficult for any faction to see to it that, at every moment in the changing course of events, it had exactly the treaties that would be advantageous. There would be abundant opportunities to be mistaken: to overestimate one threat and underestimate another; to be taken by surprise in a realignment of alliances; to see violation where there is compliance or compliance where there is violation; to think it open season on some weakling, unaware that your treaty partner regards that weakling as an ally. Too much care not to tolerate deplorable opinions without an adequate *quid pro quo* is unwise, if it makes the whole arrangement unworkable. Then the desired protection cannot be had.

There might instead be one big simple treaty, loose in its terms, prescribing indiscriminate toleration all around. Exceptions to a treaty of toleration—for the weak, for the intolerant, or for the extra-dangerous—seem at first to make sense. But they threaten to wreck the treaty. As new opinionated factions arise, and old ones wax and wane and merge and split, there will be occasion for endless doubt and haggling about what the exceptions do and don't cover. If some suppression is a violation and some falls under the exceptions, then the first can be masked as the second and the second can be misperceived as the first; all the more so, if most of the cases that arise are unclear ones. Then who can know how well the treaty is really working? How confident can anyone be that his own toleration will be reciprocated in the cases that matter? It will be all too easy to doubt whether it makes good sense to remain in compliance.

Therefore, beware exceptions. Keep it simple, stupid—that which is not there cannot go wrong.[14] First, some toleration of dangerous opinions is justified as a *quid pro quo*; then other toleration is justified because it makes the first transaction feasible.

Ought we to say, simply: *no* exceptions? It seems as if an exception that works even-handedly, and not to the permanent disadvantage of any opinion, ought to be safe. If we regulate only the manner of expression and not the content, why should anybody think that he has nothing to reciprocate because his own opinion is beyond toleration? Nobody has an opinion that he can express only by falsely shouting fire in a theatre, or only by defamation, or only by obscenity. Yet we know that even such exceptions as these can be abused. Some clever analogiser will try to erase the line between the innocent even-handed exception and the dangerous discriminatory one. He will claim that denouncing conscription is like shouting fire in a theatre, because both create a clear and present danger. Or he will claim that sharp criticism of the conduct of high officials is defamatory. Or he will claim that common smut is not half so obscene as the disgusting opinions of his opponent. If we put any limit to toleration, it is not enough to make sure that the line as drawn will not undermine the treaty. We also need some assurance that the line will stay in place where it was drawn, and not shift under pressure.

No exceptions are altogether safe; maybe some are safe enough. That is a question only to be answered by experience, and experience seems to show that some exceptions—the few we have now—are safe enough. They have not yet undermined the treaty, despite all the efforts of mischievous analogisers, and there is no obvious reason why they should become more dangerous in future. We needn't fear them much, and perhaps we can even welcome such benefits as they bring. But to try out some new and different exceptions would be foolhardy.

A simple, nearly exceptionless, well-established treaty of toleration could in time become not just a constraint of conduct, but a climate of thought. If, in the end, you will always decide that the balance of cost and benefit comes out in favour of complying with the treaty, why should you ever stop to think about the harm done by tolerating a dangerous error? Eventually you will be tolerant by habit, proudly, cheerfully, and without thought of the costs: You will proceed as if the neutralist tally were the whole story about the costs and benefits of suppression. You will bracket whatever you may think about the harm done by others' opinions. You might still think, in some compartment of your mind, that certain opinions are false and harmful. If the treaty of toleration has become second nature, you might be hard put to explain why these opinions are not dangerous enough to be worth suppressing. But you will never think of the danger as any reason to suppress.

This habit of bracketing might be not just a consequence of a treaty but part of its very content. Not so if the treaty is a formal one, to be sure; that had better regulate action, not thought, so that it can be exact and verifiable enough to permit confident agreement. But insofar as the treaty is an informal understanding, uncodified, growing up gradually, it may prescribe not only tolerant conduct but also habits of thought conducive to toleration. In particular, it may prescribe bracketing. If your compartmentalised habits of thoughts are to some extent within your control—not indeed at every moment, but at those moments when you don't bother to think things through as thoroughly as you might—then you may compartmentalise for a utilitarian reason. You may see, dimly, that when you bracket your fear of others' dangerous opinions, you participate in a custom that serves utility by your lights because it protects opinions you deem beneficial, and that would not long persist if the bracketing that conduces to toleration were not mostly reciprocated.

If a treaty of toleration tends to turn us into Milquetoasts and Millians, that is not wholly a bad thing. It is too bad if we become compartmentalised in our thinking, repressing at some times what we believe at other times about the harm opinions can do. But if we forget the costs of toleration, that makes toleration more robust. And if toleration is beneficial on balance, the more robust the better.

13. Conclusion

What is toleration good for? A proper utilitarian answer need not omit the neutralist tally. After all, it does carry some weight in favour of toleration. But the principal part of the answer cannot be neutral. The main benefit of toleration is that it protects so-and-so particular opinions, true and beneficial, which would be in danger of suppression were it not for the institutions of toleration. When reciprocal toleration protects such-and-such other opinions, false and harmful, that is a cost to be regretted, and not to be denied. When a utilitarian favours toleration, of course, it is because he reckons that the benefits outweigh the costs.

If you think it would serve utility to 'withdraw tolerance' from such-and-such dangerous opinions, you'd better think through *all* the consequences. Your effort might be an ineffective gesture; in which case, whatever you might accomplish, you will not do away with the danger. Or it might be not so ineffective. To the extent that you succeed in withdrawing toleration from your enemy, to that extent you deprive him of his incentive to tolerate you. If toleration is withdrawn in *all* directions, are you sure the opinions that enhance utility will be better off? When we no longer renounce the *argumentum ad baculum*, are you sure it will be you that carries the biggest stick?[15]

Notes

1. John Stuart Mill, *On Liberty* (London: J. W. Parker & son, 1859); page references here are to the edition edited by C. V. Shields (Indianapolis: Bobbs-Merrill, 1956).

2. Another possibility is that the means of suppression might be turned to a new purpose which, like the original suppression, serves utility according to the opinions of some but not of others. The Informer of Bray, like the Vicar, might serve his new masters as willingly as he served the old. But this danger, however weighty it might seem to some, is inadmissible under the rule of neutralism.

3. H. J. McCloskey, 'The State and Evil', *Ethics* 69 (1959), p. 190; W. V. Quine, *Quiddities An Intermittently Philosophical Dictionary* (Cambridge, Massachusetts: Harvard University Press, 1987), p. 208.

4. Spoken by the just and wise inquisitor in George Bernard Shaw, *Saint Joan* (London: Constable, 1924), p. 77.

5. Here I follow C. L. Ten, *Mill on Liberty* (Oxford: Clarendon Press, 1980), pp. 124–127, in distinguishing Mill's 'Avoidance of Mistake Argument' from his 'Assumption of Infallibility Argument'.

6. 'Repressive Tolerance' in R. P. Wolff, B. Moore, and H. Marcuse, eds., *A Critique of Pure Tolerance* (Boston: Beacon Press, 1965), p. 109.

7. *The Remarkable Birth of Planet Earth* (San Diego: Creation-Life Publishers, 1972), p. 75.

8. *Scientific Creationism* (San Diego: Creation-Life Publishers, 1974), p. 178.

9. H. T. Webster, *The Best of H. T. Webster: A Memorial Collection* (New York: Simon and Schuster, 1953), pp. 158–185.

10. Milquetoast may resemble the sort of liberal portrayed in Thomas Nagel. 'Moral Conflict and Political Legitimacy', *Philosophy & Public Affairs* 16 (1987), pp. 215–240: 'The defense of liberalism requires that a limit somehow be drawn to appeals to *the truth* in political argument' (p 227). True liberalism 'must depend on a distinction between what justifies individual belief and what justified appealing to that belief in support of the exercise of political power' (p. 229). But of course Nagel's liberal is moved not by timidity but by high principle.

11. I shall be speaking almost as if there were a conflict of opposed aims. Strictly speaking, there is not. Both sides are, *ex hypothesi*, wholehearted in their pursuit of utility. But their fundamental disagreement about how to pursue their common aim is no different, strategically, from a fundamental conflict of aims. We may speak for short of a gain for one side, versus a gain for the other. But what that really means is a gain for utility according to the opinion of one side, versus a gain for utility according to the opinion of the other.

12. Formal treaties of toleration, specifically between Catholic and Protestant powers, played a great part in the origins of the institutions of toleration we know today. But we can very well question whether those treaties were equilibria in the pursuit of utility in the largest sense, or whether they were just an escape from the horrors of war in the short term.

13. Unfortunately, a parallel case might be made out for a treaty that not only enjoins toleration between the orthodox and the heretics, but also bans proselytising. That might offer the orthodox their best hope for preventing the slow and peaceful extinction of orthodoxy, and likewise offer the heretics their best hope for preventing the slow and peaceful extinction of heresy. It would be bad for toleration, since each side would have to sustain the treaty by curbing its own zealots. But while this might be a third equilibrium, preferred both to war and to toleration with proselytising, it needn't be. Only if neither side has much confidence in its powers of persuasion will it be an equilibrium at all, let alone a preferred one.

14. The second half is quoted from the instructions for a Seagull outboard motor.

15. I thank audiences on several occasions for helpful discussions. Thanks are due especially to D. M. Armstrong, Geoffrey Brennan, Keith Campbell, Philip Kitcher, Martin Krygier, Stephanie Lewis, Michael Mahoney, Thomas Nagel, H. J. McCloskey, T. M. Scanlon, D. W. Skubik, and Kim Sterelny.

2

John Stuart Mill and the Harm of Pornography

David Dyzenhaus

Introduction

Many feminists argue that pornography should be censored because it harms women.[1] While there is growing opposition to this procensorship position within feminism, [2] it is liberals who resist censorship as a matter of principle. In this essay, I suggest that liberals should not adopt a stance of principled opposition to censoring pornography.

This liberal stance is made up of three main ingredients.[3] First, liberals argue that the state is entitled to intervene coercively in individuals' lives on the basis of a narrow harm principle which permits governments so to act only in order to protect the physical integrity of individuals. Since the evidence that pornography causes attacks on physical integrity is nowhere near conclusive, liberals suppose that pornography generally satisfies harmless male preferences. The harm principle cannot justify coercion in this case.[4]

Second, liberals argue that the consumption of pornography is a matter of private, as opposed to public, morality. Liberals are committed to protecting the private because they want to respect a right of individual autonomy. The state must allow individuals maximum space in which to live according to their own lights. For liberals, consumption of pornography is, in a famous phrase of the Wolfenden Report, "not the law's business,"[5] at least when it is produced by consenting adults for adult consumption in private.[6]

Third, liberals are committed to a right of complete freedom of expression, which makes them hostile to any censorship whatsoever. Either they suppose that expression, as opposed to conduct, cannot harm individuals in a manner which would justify state or other coercion, or they suppose that attempts to regulate expression invariably result in greater harm than the harm which particular acts of expression might cause.

For procensorship feminists, the liberal refusal to censor pornography shows the poverty of liberalism. In particular, it exposes the inability of liberalism to deal with one of the chief defects of contemporary society—the subordination of women to men. This understanding of pornography holds that in our society relations between women and men are profoundly unequal because they occur in a context in which women are in a state of social, political, and personal subjection to men. If we examine pornography in this context, we will understand it as an integral and important part of a regime of subordination which is rooted ultimately in superior physical force.

It is not that procensorship feminists object to sexually explicit depictions per se. They emphasize that it is not the sexual explicitness of the depiction or description that makes an item pornographic. For them pornography is the portrayal of women as the perpetual objects of male sexual desires. Pornography is pornography not because of its sexual character but because of the context of inequality which it eroticizes. The characteristic which demarcates pornography from other kinds of patriarchal expression is that it makes inequality seem sexy.

Much pornography is explicitly violent. It shows men forcing women into sex of a more or less brutal nature. But for procensorship feminists that kind of pornography is but one end of a continuum, the other end of which is pornography showing women consenting to and enjoying their role in satisfying male sexual desires. These feminists think that such "consensual" pornography is as much a matter for concern as violent pornography.

They point out that actual relationships of inequality between men and women exist on the same continuum as pornography, from relationships of subordination which are maintained by brute force to those which appear consensual. And it is the portrayal of consent, not of force and coercion, that legitimizes inequality and subordination. "Consensual" pornography makes the inequality that already exists between men and women appear legitimate as well as sexy. Moreover, the particular character of pornography is that its consumption generally takes place in private, in the same place as much of the relationship of subordination of women to men is acted out.

The harm of pornography is then the special way in which it contributes to a regime of inequality. That regime prevents women from articulating and living out conceptions of the good life which would be theirs to explore were they in a position of substantive equality. It is not that procensorship feminists think that eradicating pornography will bring about the end of patriarchal inequality; but they seem to suppose that the eradication would affect a wider group than the consumers of pornography. If done appropriately, the eradication would be a message to women as well as to men that inequality is neither desirable nor legitimate. A pernicious prop of inequality; one which combines a complex message about inequality and desire, force and consent, would be removed.[7]

In this article, I will not engage directly in the contemporary debate between liberals and feminists about pornography.[8] I want to ask what John Stuart Mill might have said about the topic of pornography.[9] It might seem that the answer to this question is obvious. After all, the ingredients of the principled liberal opposition to censoring pornography appear to have their roots in *On Liberty*: in Mill's articulation of a narrow harm principle as the sole legitimate basis for state coercion; in his zeal to protect a private sphere of "self-regarding" action for the sake of an ideal of individual autonomy of self-government; and in his defense of a right to complete freedom of expression.[10] But I will suggest that liberals who regard Mill as the founder of their tradition should reevaluate their position on pornography in the light of Mill's curiously neglected essay *The Subjection of Women*.[11]

I will argue, first, that a proper appreciation of *The Subjection of Women* shows that Mill would have been surprisingly sympathetic to the procensorship feminist case. What then of the ingredients that make up the principled liberal opposition to censorship?

I address this question in the second part of the article, arguing that the considerations which would make Mill sympathetic to the procensorship feminist case are not in conflict with the major arguments of *On Liberty*. We will then have grounds to question a principled liberal opposition to censoring pornography.

The Subjection of Women

Mill's opening statement in *The Subjection of Women* was radical by the standards of his day. He will argue, he says, that the legal regime of his day which subordinates women to men is "wrong in itself, . . . one of the chief hindrances to human improvement," and that it "ought to be replaced by a principle of perfect equality, admitting no power or privilege on the one side, nor disability on the other" (*SW*, p. 261).

His statement might seem mild in contemporary liberal democracies, which, however much they might disagree about what equality requires, are committed to attaining it formally for all. Thus they have eradicated by and large the legal disabilities which subordinated women in Mill's time. What remains radical today is Mill's analysis of the nature of women's subordination, one which explains why, despite a legal order characterized by formal commitments to equality, feminists still find that substantive equality of women with men remains a dim prospect.

Mill's stated aim is to argue against the legal subordination of women and for what he calls "perfect equality." But he clearly does not equate absence of legally prescribed inequality with presence of substantive equality. For one thing, Mill does not see legally prescribed inequalities between men and women as much more than the de jure recognition of de facto social relationships based ultimately on what he regards as the root cause of subordination—the superior physical power of males (*SW*, p. 264). Thus the more pressing need is to deal with the social relationships. In addition, while Mill sees the legal victories that would be won were women admitted to the suffrage and were the laws of marriage and divorce radically reformed as essential steps toward the goal of perfect equality, the victories are, given his understanding of the marks of women's inequality, far from sufficient.

The first mark of women's inequality is that it cuts across class boundaries. Power over women is "common to the whole male sex" and jealously guarded since, Mill claims, power over those closest to us seems particularly valuable given that it is those closest to us who are in a position to interfere more with our preferences (*SW*, p. 268). The second mark, which explains the persistence of this power and the certainty of its outlasting "all other forms of unjust authority" is that the power is generally exercised in the privacy and intimacy of the home. This private nature of the power prevents women from combining to articulate their common experience of their subjection. Indeed, says Mill, it is surprising that the "protests and testimony against it have been so numerous and weighty as they are" (*SW*, pp. 268–69).

The third mark is the apparent naturalness of the relationship of inequality. Mill notes that every relationship of domination appears natural to the dominators (*SW*, pp. 269–70). He also notes that subjected classes often appear to accept their subjection as the natural order of things, since even in their initial struggle against domination they complain not "of the power itself but only of its oppressive exercise." And he points out in this regard that women who do complain of the abuse by men of their power suffer uniquely (with children) in being "replaced under the physical power of the culprit" (*SW*, p. 271).[12]

Mill wants to draw attention to the especially insidious quality of this mark of power. That quality is one which men want and one which they succeed in exacting—having women as their "willing slaves." It is important to spend some time on Mill's analysis of this idea. Men, he says, desire of women more than the obedience which, say, fear of coercion or religious fear might exact from a subject class. This is because the women over whom they most want to exercise power are "most nearly connected with them." What they require, and what they have contrived to acquire, is a morality combined with a sentimentality which will make it the feminine ideal to be placed in a relationship of subjection to a man. To this end, women are educated to believe that their character is the "very opposite to that of men; not self-will, and government by self-control, but submission, and yielding to the control of others." The morality tells them that this is their duty and the sentimentality that it is their nature "to live for others; make complete abnegations of themselves, and to have not life but in their affections," that is, their affections for their husbands and children. If we take together the fact of what Mill calls the "natural attraction between opposite sexes," the "woman's entire dependence on the husband," and that all her social ambition has to be realized through him, "it would be a miracle if the object of being attractive to men had not become the polar star of feminine education and formation of character" (*SW*, pp. 271–72).[13]

So for Mill the fact that women, or at least many of them, willingly accept their social condition does not detract from the coercive nature of their relationship with men. Indeed, the coercion involved is in a way worse than slavery since what is in fact a relationship of forced inequality is made to appear consensual.[14]

In sum, for Mill the subjection of women comes about because of a status quo of inequality, which is made most manifest in the private realm and which is made to look natural by a false appearance of consent. And what is pernicious about this regime of inequality is that it prevents women from acting as autonomous individuals, from articulating and exploring their own conceptions of the good life. For it is the promise of autonomy that Mill takes to the distinctive of what he calls "the peculiar character of the modern world": that "human beings are no longer born to their place in life, and chained down by an inexorable bond to the place they are born to, but are free to employ their faculties, and such favourable chances as offer, to achieve the lot which may appear to them most desirable" (*SW*, pp. 272–73).

If pornography does eroticize inequality, the very circumstances which Mill identifies as the subjection of women are what makes pornography a harm. Pornography is consumed in a private realm. It makes an inequality which is ultimately rooted in superior physical power and thus in physical coercion appear sexually desirable. And, at the same time, it attempts to legitimize itself by claiming the consent of women to their subordination. That is, by eroticizing inequality, pornography plays a special role in sustaining the regime of inequality—the regime which prevents women from articulating and living out conceptions of the good life which rival those that patriarchy rules appropriate.

The crucial move for Mill, the one which brings his understanding of the subjection of women into line with the procensorship feminist understanding of the harm of pornography, is his willingness to deem coercive what has the appearance of consent. In effect, he invokes an idea of false consciousness.

So it seems that if procensorship feminists are right about pornography, Mill would not be sympathetic to an appeal to the consensual nature of either the production or the consumption of pornography. Liberals can make that appeal as part of their justification for opposing censorship of pornography, because the appearance of consent seems to show that pornography satisfies certain harmless male sexual preferences. That women participate in the production of pornography and in the fantasies of men who consume pornography is taken as evidence of the absence of harm. But on Mill's account of subjection, the consent of women to be featured in pornography, and the consent of women to live out the ideas about women's nature which pornography supplies for its consumers, might be entirely manufactured. If so, pornography is especially pernicious because the appearance of consent is given to a deeply coercive relationship.

This conclusion will seem problematic to liberals, especially to those in the Millian tradition. The hallmark of Millian liberalism is taken by both liberals and their critics to be its utilitarian, "want-regarding character"—that is, its respect for people's actual preferences—what appears to them to be good.[15] Whatever liberals think people would desire if they had an understanding of what is really in their interests, liberalism is supposed to be legitimately concerned only with what people take their interests and wants to be. For example, Steven Lukes, in his illuminating monograph on power, argues that liberals, because of their reliance on actual wants, are barred from adopting a radical conception of power which maintains that people's "wants may themselves be a product of a system which works against their interests, and, in such cases, relates the latter to what they would want and prefer, were they able to make the choice."[16]

The puzzle for Mill is then to provide a reconciliation of his concern for what in fact appears to the willing slaves as most desirable—as their "polar star"—with what he thinks they would desire, had they an understanding of what is really in their interests.

Nature and Experience

Mill's solution to the puzzle is found in his complex account of experience as the testing ground for valid observations about human nature. At the very outset of *The Subjection of Women* he says that the authority of men over women would have some claim as a justifiable regime only if it were thought to be so "on the testimony of experience." But for this to be so, women and men must have experienced social life under conditions of perfect equality. Only then could the system of subordination be said to be "conducive to the happiness and well-being of both [sexes]" (*SW*, p. 263). As he puts it, "Experience cannot possibly have decided between two courses, so long as there has only been experience of one" (*SW*, p. 276).

To a large extent, then, Mill's appeal to experience is not to actual but to potential experience. An appeal to actual experience is illicit in this case because actual experience is not merely incomplete, it is also contaminated. Women and men have been denied the benefit of experience which they would have had were women not the passive victims of a regime which reproduces them with a nature suited to the selfish and exploitative interests of men. Indeed, Mill denies that we can have knowledge of the nature of either sex, because of the one-sided nature of previous experience. In particular, he says of women's nature that it is "an eminently artificial thing—the result of forced repression in some directions, unnatural stimulation in others." Women have experienced a "hot-house and stove cultivation . . . carried on of some of the capabilities of their nature, for the benefit and pleasure of their masters" (*SW*, p. 276). Even men who do achieve truly affectionate relationships with their spouses cannot know them, for even the best of relationships will be contaminated by the overarching context of subjection (*SW*, pp. 278–79).[17]

How then is knowledge of women's nature to be revealed? It can be revealed, Mill thinks, only when women are liberated from the regime of inequality which silences them. "We can safely assert that the knowledge which men can acquire of women, even as they have been and are, without reference to what they might be, is wretchedly imperfect and superficial, and always will be so, until women themselves have told all that they have to tell" (*SW*, pp. 278–79).[18]

Mill could be understood as supposing here that women need to discover their true nature under conditions of perfect equality, because such knowledge is a prerequisite for women successfully to articulate and to explore a conception of the good life. Alternatively, in line with his remarks about the self-serving aspects of claims about naturalness, Mill could be understood as saying that claims about an inherent human nature should at any time be regarded with some suspicion.

However, Mill is barred by his radicalism from himself deciding between these alternatives. As he tells us, knowledge of women's nature is not "necessary for any practical purpose," since, in accordance with the principle which he claims as the guiding ideal of modern society, "that question rests with women themselves—to be decided by their own experience, and by the use of their own faculties" (*SW*, p. 280).

In addition, in the context of his discussion of the subjection of women Mill does not have to opt for either option. For him our present views of women's nature have no standing because what we take as natural is in fact the construct of a regime of inequality. His direct concern is not with the issue of whether women have or could be said to have a nature, but with the suspect use of a claim about their nature to legitimize a regime of inequality. Since any such claim cannot be tested except under conditions of equality, he can focus on the fact that women are prevented from articulating and exploring conceptions of the good life by a regime of inequality.

If Mill has any bias on the issue of nature, it is that men and women will discover, under the right conditions, that they share an interest in leading autonomous lives.[19] He supposes that, insofar as the modern world has experienced autonomy and the progress toward equality which is its condition, that experience has proved beneficial (*SW*, p. 276). His project has been well-described as an "empirical wager."[20] He predicts that his opinion will be vindicated if it is given the opportunity provided by adopting an agnostic position on the topic of women's nature.

In sum, Mill's solution to the puzzle about real and perceived interests and wants is the following. If one's concern is individual autonomy, and if there is reason to suppose that a group's wants were formed under a regime hostile to autonomy, one cannot appeal to those wants to justify the regime. On Mill's construal of utilitarianism, there is not merely a contingent connection between individuality and welfare. His basic utilitarian message is that something cannot count as in my interest unless my assessment of it is achieved under conditions of autonomy, or real control over my life choices.[21] And this conclusion supports a procensorship case, which claims that eradicating pornography is in the real interests of men as well as women.

However, while this solution to the puzzle about real interests is Mill's, it might still be rejected as one repugnant to Millian liberals who take their cues from *On Liberty*. As I have pointed out, the arguments of *On Liberty* are taken to support a principled liberal opposition to censorship. These are the arguments for a narrow harm principle which permits governments to use coercion only to protect individuals from assaults on physical integrity, for a right of autonomy against state intrusions into the area of private morality, and for a right to complete freedom of expression. So there appears to be a fundamental tension in Mill's political theory. The tension is dissolved, I shall argue, if *The Subjection of Women* is read as the authoritative text with which *On Liberty* should cohere.

The Harm Principle

Critics of liberalism often complain about what appears to them to be a liberal obsession with limiting the power of the state to coerce individuals. The ground of this complaint is that the state does not have a monopoly of power. Classes and groups also have and exercise power; and a position which seeks to limit state coercion alone must perpetuate by default existing and often pernicious power relations.

But should *On Liberty* be read, as it often is by both liberals and their critics, as the source of the liberal focus on the evils of state coercion? Not if one takes Mill's opening statement at face value. He says that his concern in the essay is the "nature and limits of the power which can be legitimately exercised *by society* over the individual" (*OL*, p. 217; my emphasis). Of course Mill sees that power is exercised by enacting and enforcing legislation. And he is concerned about the potential in an age of representative government for majorities to use legislation as a means to impose illegitimately their conceptions of right and wrong on minorities. But his main concern remains what he calls "social tyranny," which he describes as "more formidable than many kinds of political oppression, since, though not usually upheld by such extreme penalties, it leaves fewer means of escape, penetrating much more deeply into the details of life, and enslaving the soul itself" (*OL*, p. 220). Mill's point here is that while the penalties attached to political oppression are extreme, the oppression itself is overt and thus transparent to the oppressed. By contrast, social oppression is disguised by our habituation to it, even by our apparent consent to oppression when our very souls become enslaved.

The question, as Mill sees it, concerns the limit to both "physical force in the form of legal penalties" and "the moral coercion of public opinion." His famous answer is what has since been dubbed the "harm principle": that "the only purpose for which power can be exercised over any member of a civilized community, against his will, is to prevent harm to others. . . . His own good is . . . not a sufficient warrant. The only part of the conduct of any one, for which he is amenable to society, is that which con-

cerns others. In the part which merely concerns himself, his inde-
pendence is, of right, absolute" (*OL*, pp. 223–24). This claim,
Mill says, is grounded in utility—the "permanent interests of
man as a progressive being" (*OL*, p. 224).

Mill sometimes talks of the harm principle as involving self-
protection,[22] thus conjuring up an image of protection from
physical assaults of various kinds. And such talk leads, of course,
to the traditional, narrow harm principle: the state is entitled to
intervene coercively in individuals' lives only to protect the physical integrity of individuals. But as the extracts quoted above tell
us, he is concerned not only with physical assaults, nor only with
the coercive power of the state; he is also concerned with the
"moral coercion" exercised by powerful groups. And his analysis
of the subjection of women seems to identify the power exercised
by men over women through pornography as a pernicious kind of
social and moral coercion.

Mill's concern with social coercion might seem to give rise to
the following interpretation of the harm principle: powerful
groups must not coerce individuals unless this is to prevent harm.
It would follow that if pornography is a kind of coercive power, it
would be illegitimate unless it could be shown to prevent harm.
For reasons to be explored below, I think that Mill does want to
reserve the monopoly of legitimate force to the state. That is, his
concern with social or moral coercion is not to limit such coercion
by the harm principle, but to point out the existence of such coercion. Mill wants us to be alert for the harm of coercion even, perhaps especially, when there is no assault on physical integrity and
the coercion is masked by the fact that its victims appear to consent to the regime under which they live. And, as I have already
argued, in *The Subjection of Women* Mill sees the need to rest his
analysis of coercion on a conception of real interests.

In fact, he makes it clear in *On Liberty* that his conception of
harm is interest-based. He says that apart from protection from
the harm of assaults, people are entitled to protection from harm
to their interests, "or rather certain interests, which, either by
express legal provision or by tacit understanding ought to be considered as rights. . . . As soon as any part of a person's conduct

affects prejudicially the interests of others, society has jurisdiction over it, and the question whether the general welfare will or will not be promoted by interfering with it, becomes open to discussion" (*OL*, p. 276).

In my view, Mill clearly did not intend that the interests that deserve protection should be confined to those which individuals happen to think deserve protection.[23] Besides the fact that he speaks of interests which "ought" to be considered as rights, there is the consideration that in writing *On Liberty* he is motivated by a clearly articulated fear that what he regards as the "permanent interests of man as a progressive being" are both not generally recognized in his day and in danger of being swamped by moralistic majoritarianism.[24] That is to say, *On Liberty* is written in order to combat a predominant, growing, and false conception of interest.

Thus Mill's understanding of harm is normative insofar as one of the harms he is most concerned about is harm to the interest individuals have in autonomy. He clearly sees that the practices of a moralistic majority can be as coercive and as harmful to that interest as any state action. His own account in *The Subjection of Women* of the way in which patriarchy subordinates women shows that he considered patriarchy to amount to just such a coercive practice. And, as we have seen, his analysis of the subjection of women supports a claim that he would have been open to understanding pornography as social or moral coercion.

In sum, I want to suggest that the right interpretation of Mill's harm principle is the following: governments must not coerce individuals unless their conduct is harmful in the broad sense that includes prejudice to fundamental interests. And all the arguments of *On Liberty* are directed toward supporting the conclusion that among the fundamental interests of individuals, of "man as a progressive being," is the interest in autonomy.

A Right of Privacy

Given this, it would be remarkable had Mill thought that his category of "self-regarding" action committed him to the claim that we can establish a priori the boundaries of a realm of private action into which there can be no state intrusion. Indeed, his argument in this regard in *On Liberty* is as strong as that found in his discussion of the despotism of the patriarchal family in *The Subjection of Women*:[25]

> The State, while it respects the liberty of each in what especially regards himself, is bound to maintain a vigilant control over his exercise of any power which it allows him to possess over others. This obligation is almost entirely disregarded in the case of family relations, a case, in its direct influence on human happiness, more important than all others taken together. The almost despotic power of husbands over wives need not be enlarged upon here, because nothing more is needed for the complete removal of the evil, than that wives should have the same rights, and should receive the protection of law in the same manner, as all other persons. [OL, p. 301]

As Gail Tulloch has pointed out, to take this idea seriously requires "interferences in family life which go beyond what has been done in most liberal states, including taking strong action against violence in families and rape in marriage."[26]

So, since for Mill the area of self-regarding activity is that which one has on condition that one does not in public or in private harm the essential interests of others, the question of whether pornography should be regarded as falling into this area cannot be answered in advance by a public/private distinction.

The Right to Freedom of Expression

This leaves the issue of Mill's defense in chapter 2 of *On Liberty* of a right to an apparently complete freedom of expression. I want to suggest that Mill's understanding of the right to freedom of expression is not as absolutist as is commonly thought. It is sufficiently complex to permit what we might think of as a liberal censorship policy.

In *On Liberty*, Mill does express a general aversion to "forcing improvements on an unwilling people" in the cause of a "spirit of improvement." So we might suppose that persuasion through speech is the only means he would countenance for getting rid of pornography (*OL*, p. 272). Is it that Mill should believe that the "real solvent of public morality" is debate so that his hope is that truth will emerge merely from "free critical discussion"?[27]

The answer to this last question must surely be "no," if we take seriously Mill's account of the subjection of women. For we have seen in Mill's link between women's silence and their lack of autonomy that the very space of discussion is crimped and distorted by an oppressive regime. I think that *On Liberty* can support this answer if we notice a distinction between two methods by which a public debate might be said to control a "spirit of improvement" which aims to control the coercive power of pornographic speech.

On the first method, one hopes debate has this control merely because one hopes that indefinite and uncontrolled conversation will eventually reveal the truth. But any coercive restraints on complete freedom of expression are ruled out. The hope is thus that individuals whose conceptions of the good life contain elements collectively constitutive of oppression will come to recognize that they should reform.

On the second method, debate controls a spirit of improvement in part by establishing what coercive action should be taken in order to eradicate oppressive conceptions of the good life: thus permitting, for example, the censorship of pornography.

It might seem that Mill's defense of freedom of thought and expression in chapter 2 of *On Liberty* can only support the first method. There, on the basis of our recognition of our own fallibility, he presents the following arguments. We should never suppress an opinion since it might be right. Even if we "know" an opinion is wrong, the presence of wrong opinions serves to sharpen our perception and appreciation of the truth. Since the testing ground for truth is experience, we should not constrain expression since that is to limit the experience which is our only ground of determining truth. Thus we cannot impose an opinion on others even if we think that we have sufficient warrant for thinking it true. These arguments are linked to Mill's doctrine that individuals should be left alone to conduct their own experiments in living, since it is through public expression that individuals will learn of the variety of experiments undertaken by others. He says that the "peculiar evil of silencing the expression of an opinion is, that it is robbing the human race; . . . those who dissent from the opinion, still more than those who hold it" (*OL*, p. 229).

However, this first method seems to presuppose that expression, by contrast with conduct, cannot harm. And there is no evidence in *On Liberty* of Mill holding to a distinction between expression and conduct such that expression is by stipulation incapable of amounting to conduct harmful to others and thus incapable of justifying coercive action. Consider his much discussed distinction between (legitimately) publishing a newspaper article which says that corn dealers are "starvers of the poor" and (illegitimately) saying the same to an angry mob (*OL*, p. 259). That distinction entails that an opinion becomes harmful conduct in a context where its expression threatens interests which require coercive protection. And the pro-censorship, feminist claim about pornography is that once pornography is understood in the overarching context of women's subordination and inequality, it will be seen as a mode of conduct which plays a special role in maintaining inequality.

Moreover, in chapter 2 of *On Liberty* Mill often speaks of conduct as a form of expression. It would be odd for him to talk otherwise, since his discussion of freedom of expression, when read in the context of *On Liberty* as a whole, is mainly about the importance of individuals being exposed to different experiments in living to give them the resources to engage in experiments of their own. And given the weight Mill attaches in that chapter to learning from actual experience, it is important for him that individual exposure is not merely to beliefs about how to live, but to conduct that amounts to living that way.[28]

And if pornography eroticizes inequality, a question about coercive intervention by the state is raised which cannot be settled by a conduct/expression distinction. For in the light of Mill's understanding of experience in *The Subjection of Women*, we need to take into account the thought that certain kinds of expression produce experience which is not an adequate testing ground for truth, since that experience is of a regime of inequality which is in fact experience-constraining.

The constraint has two aspects: it constrains the experience of inquiry itself—it silences the articulation of possible experiences—and it prevents from coming into existence actual experience of what it would be like to live those possibilities. To allow this kind of experience to be one's testing ground is to permit an ongoing process of self-validation of an oppressive ideology. One cannot appeal to Mill's dictum that silencing an opinion is an evil when the issue is how to deal with an exercise of male freedom of expression which perpetuates the inequality of women.

Finally, Mill argues in *On Liberty* that his fallibilist position does not commit one to inaction on the basis that, because one's beliefs about what is right can never be assumed to be infallible, they should never be enforced. Mill does not oppose acting on the basis of opinions that have passed the tribunal of experience. He opposes assuming the truth of an opinion "for the purpose of not permitting its refutation." All that he supposes fallibilism to require is to keep the "lists" of debate open so that the action taken remains open to the scrutiny of public debate, and thus to revision (*OL*, pp. 231–32).

I suggest that this requirement indicates that Mill would have been averse to the first interpretation of the harm principle, that powerful groups can coerce individuals in order to prevent harm. Recall that Mill thinks that social or moral coercion is worse than political coercion because the coercion of the state is at least transparent. The obvious virtue of transparency is that it attracts attention and thus public scrutiny. In addition, if coercive action is going to be undertaken, it must, for Mill, be undertaken after full discussion. And giving a monopoly of legitimate force to the state will, if the state is a liberal one, ensure that state action has been subjected to full public scrutiny.

Moreover, if the legislative policy and mechanisms involved in the state action are carefully crafted so as to make it clear what is at stake—the eroticization of inequality—that policy can plausibly be said to be liberal, one which a Millian might support. The harm in eroticizing inequality is the harm to the fundamental interest we all have in autonomy. Mill's defense of freedom of expression in *On Liberty* is mainly in the service of that same interest. So liberals should squarely face the question whether limiting freedom of expression might not sometimes be justified when the limitation is in the service of, and controlled by, the value of autonomy.[29]

Conclusion

I have tried to show that Mill must be open to the legitimacy of coercive action to eradicate pornography. This does not mean that he would have opted for censorship. Like many feminists today, he might have thought that we need to know a great deal more about pornography than we do at present, or that public education is likely to be more effective and beneficial than coercion which would drive pornography underground. But then there is little or no difference in principle between him and procensorship feminists.

This conclusion follows from an interpretation of Mill which shifts his concerns about substantive equality and individual autonomy to center stage. The argument for it rests on a rich conception of harm, one which embraces harm to fundamental interests, such as the interest in an autonomous life of the kind that is achievable only under conditions of equality. The harm principle still determines which conceptions of the good life we can legitimately condemn, but the domain traditionally accorded by liberals to official neutrality must shrink. For example, the patriarchal conception of the good life is not one about which a liberal state should be neutral because its price is the inequality of women.

This conclusion should matter to liberals not only because it follows from the arguments of the thinker who is rightly regarded as the founder of contemporary liberal political theory. The conclusion also allows liberals to start to take seriously claims about social injustice which would otherwise, as a matter of principle, seem off limits to them.

The conclusion should, I think, also matter to feminists. The dominant ideologies which today vie for political power are liberalism and conservatism. While conservatives are willing to use state coercion to enforce morality, and have in fact sometimes joined with feminists in attempts to use the law to eradicate pornography,[30] their willingness is premised on what for feminists have to be wrong reasons.

Conservatives think that the use of state coercion is justified when there is a threat to what they hold to be the core values of a legitimate status quo. Thus they want to censor pornography because it offends norms which figure among standards of public decency. But similarly they want to preserve the patriarchal character of the status quo. So for feminists who regard eradicating pornography as an essential step in their struggle for women's equality, liberals, who do not have any a priori commitment to the value of the status quo, would seem better allies. And the fact that the most eminent modern liberal was able to foresee some of the main themes of a feminist account of women's inequality should be a useful resource in persuading liberal males to reevaluate their principled opposition to censorship.

A second reason why my conclusion should matter to feminists goes beyond political expediency and embraces, perhaps even unites in some important respects, both liberal and feminist concerns. Mill did not think that the advantages which would accrue from the equality of women would be confined to women. In accordance with his basic utilitarian impulse, he predicted that the advantage would be to society overall. Besides material benefits such as the addition of many individual talents to the pool of social resources, Mill emphasized the change in the quality of men's experience both of women and themselves. He thought that under conditions of perfect equality, the difference between the sexes could be explored in a way that would make the collective experience richer. That would happen because possibilities for potentially valuable individual experiments in living would become apparent which hitherto could not be articulated because of the subjection of roughly one half of humanity (*SW*, pp. 335–40).

Mill's vision seeks to unite men and women, but in a way which recognizes the value of difference and which thus preserves a social and political space for differences to become manifest and to be explored. His dream is of a "common language" in which differences could be articulated, debated, and explored without coercion.[31] It might seem like an impossible dream. But Mill expended both genius and much of a lifetime's work in looking for the right mix of practical elements which would form its basis. His discussions of freedom of speech, the art of life, the limits of state coercion, and representative government are essential parts of this endeavor and should not be ignored by anyone who would make reality of his ideal.

Notes

For very helpful comments on drafts of this article, I thank David Beatty, Andrew Kernohan, David Lampert, Patrick Macklem, Cheryl Misak, Denise Reaume, Arthur Ripstein, Wayne Sumner, Cass Sunstein, and, especially, the editors of and two anonymous referees for *Ethics*.

1. See, e.g., C. MacKinnon, *Feminism Unmodified: Discourses on Life and Law* (Cambridge, Mass.: Harvard University Press, 1987); and A. Dworkin, *Pornography: Men Posessing Women* (London: Women's Press, 1981). Although such feminists set no store by conventional methods of censorship, I use 'censorship' here as shorthand for any coercion, whether state initiated or by dint of informal public pressure, aimed at suppressing production, distribution, and consumption of pornography. As will become clear below, the claim that pornography harms might be best understood as not limited to women, since the harm of pornography is also to men, even those who are enthusiastic consumers.

2. See, e.g., A. Snitow, C. Stansell, and S. Thompson, eds., *Powers of Desire: The Politics of Sexuality* (New York: Monthly Review, 1983), sec. 6; and V. Burstyn, ed., *Women against Censorship* (Vancouver: Douglas & McIntyre, 1985).

3. See, e.g., "Pornography, Sex, and Censorship" by F. Berger. "Pornography and the Criminal Law" by J. Feinberg, and "Freedom of Expression" by T. Scanlon, collected in D. Copp and S. Wendell, eds., *Pornography and Censorship* (Buffalo, N.Y.: Prometheus Books, 1983).

4. Even the most narrow understanding of the harm principle is usually taken to justify censoring child pornography.

5. Section 61 at p. 48 of *The Wolfenden Report*, Introduction by Karl Menninger (New York: Stein & Day, 1963).

6. I do not deal in this article with the "offense principle," which many liberals enlist to justify confining distribution and consumption of pornography to the private (see, esp., J. Feinberg. *Offense to Others*, vol. 2 of *The Moral Limits of the Criminal Law* [Oxford: Oxford University Press, 1985]). Nor do I deal with the question whether there is a basis for this principle in Mill (see J. Waldron, "Mill and the Value of Moral Distress," *Political Studies* 35 [1987]: 410–23).

7. The very complexity of the pornographic message can be used as the basis for a feminist argument against censorship (see L. Williams, *Hard Core: Power, Pleasure, and the "Frenzy of the Visible"* [Berkeley: University of California Press, 1989]).

8. See R. Langton's excellent piece on just this issue, "Whose Right? Ronald Dworkin, Women, and Pornographers," *Philosophy and Public Affairs* 19 (1990): 311–59.

9. I do not deal at all with the role that Mill's own apparent discomfort with matters sexual and his Victorian prudery might have played in his attitude to pornography. (For a discussion of such issues, see B. Mazlish, *James and John Stuart Mill: Father and Son in the Nineteenth Century* (New York: Basic, 1975) pp. 328–50). My concern, as Mill's would have been, is with issues of principle.

10. J. S. Mill, *On Liberty*, in *Collected Works*, ed. J. M. Robson (Toronto: University of Toronto Press, 1977), vol. 18: hereafter cited as *OL* with pages numbers parenthetically in the text.

11. J. S. Mill, *The Subjection of Women*, in *Collected Works*, vol. 21, ed. J. M. Robson (Toronto: University of Toronto Press, 1984); hereafter cited as *SW* with page numbers parenthetically in the text. One reason for the neglect is that feminists who find little of value in the tradition of contemporary liberal thought lack incentive to spend time on the work of the thinker who founded that tradition. Contemporary liberals have neglected the essay mainly because they regard it as a mere application of the arguments of *On Liberty*. Moreover, it might seem to them that specific reforms which the essay advocates have all been won. Thus A. Ryan, *J. S. Mill* (London: Routledge & Kegan Paul, 1974), says that the *The Subjection of Women* "is almost entirely concerned with the legal disabilities of women in Victorian England" (p. 125). H. J. McCloskey, *J. S. Mill: A Critical Study* (London: Macmillan, 1971), says that Mill's essay reads like a "series of truisms," a view which he holds because he also thinks that equality of the sexes has been achieved (p. 136). See also R. Wollheim's remarks in his introduction to *John Stuart Mill: Three Essays* (Oxford: Oxford University Press, 1984), p. xxv. An important exception is F. R. Berger, *Happiness, Justice, and Freedom: The Moral and Political Philosophy of John Stuart Mill* (Berkeley: University of California Press, 1984), pp. 195–204. The main extended philosophical treatments of which I am aware are by feminists. See J. Annas, "Mill and the Subjection of Women," *Philosophy* 52 (1977): 179–94; S. Moller Okin, *Women in Western Political Thought* (Princeton, N.J.: Princeton University Press, 1979), chap. 9: and, esp., G. Tulloch, *Mill and Sex Equality* (Hemel Hempstead: Harvester Wheatsheaf, 1989).

12. See *SW*, pp. 287–88, for further discussion. As Annas points out, Mill's point does not lose its force because battered wives are no longer legally compelled to return to their husbands so long as de facto social pressures bring about the same result (p.170). In fact, in line with Mill's argument below, we should see that the persistence of de facto social pressures in the absence of legal constraints will make things worse: for it will appear that women consent to return to the abusive situation about which they complained.

13. Compare *On Liberty*, pp. 229–301, where, in a passage which has caused some difficulty to commentators, he says that one cannot consent to slavery.

14. It is worth noting Mill's remark in this regard, which anticipates Virginia Woolf's plea for a "Room of One's Own." Mill says that Uncle Tom, under his first master, "had his own life in his 'cabin' . . . but it cannot be so with the wife" (*SW*, pp. 284–85).

15. For the term "want-regarding character," see B. Barry, *Political Argument* (London: Routledge & Kegan Paul, 1965), pp. 41–42.

16. Steven Lukes, *Power: A Radical View* (London: Macmillan, 1977), p. 34.

17. Mill's claim here is in line with some of the most radical feminist thought which says that all heterosexual relations are on a continuum, one pole of which is constituted by relations involving overt violence. For example, when he describes the marriage relationship of his day, he does not assert more than that there are extreme cases

David Dyzenhaus

which reach what he calls the "lowest abysses." But he says that there is a "sad succession of depth after depth before reaching them" (SW, p. 288).

18. Because of Mill's emphasis on the importance of the articulation of experience, he would, I think, have been more receptive than many contemporary liberals to the kind of evidence presented by feminists to show the harm of pornography. For liberals have tended to require unattainable hard statistical correlations between sexual assaults and pornography, while feminists rely mainly on the stories women have to tell about men who see them as interchangeable with the women portrayed in pornography (see, e.g., the evidence presented at the Minneapolis hearings, collected in Everywoman, *Pornography and Sexual Violence: Evidence of the Links* [London: Everywoman Ltd., 1988]).

19. See Tulloch, pp. 121–61, for a careful discussion of this issue.

20. Ibid., p. 147.

21. Mill's discussion of a distinction between "higher" and "lower" pleasures in *Utilitarianism* lends substantial support to my argument. He introduces this distinction in order to elaborate his claim that people will in fact discriminate appropriately between experiences that are the product of a life lived in accordance with a true conception of interests and a life that is lived in accordance with a false conception. He insists that the validity of such a distinction can only be judged by those who have had the experience of both kinds of pleasure. See J. S. Mill, *Utilitarianism*, in *Collected Works*, vol. 10, pp. 211–13. See also Tulloch, pp. 138–45; and see Berger, *Happiness, Justice, and Freedom*, pp. 201–4, who criticizes the understanding of Mill's utilitarianism in Annas.

22. For example, in his first full statement of the harm principle (OL, pp. 223–24).

23. Mill scholars divide on this question. Contrast, e.g., J. C. Rees, *John Stuart Mill's "On Liberty"* (Oxford: Clarendon, 1989), pp. 150–55; with J. Gray, *Mill on Liberty: A Defence* (London: Routledge & Kegan Paul, 1983), p. 50.

24. See p. 275.

25. Okin, *Women in Western Political Thought*, chap. 9, focuses on Mill's assumption that the family with its customary division of labor will be the central institution of the new, just society. Like Annas, she concludes that Mill's feminism, because it is shaped by liberal assumptions, cannot escape the status quo of patriarchy. For example, she takes Mill's suggestion that the family, while presently a "school of despotism" would when justly constituted be "the real school of the virtues of freedom" as evidence of his allegiance to a patriarchal status quo (SW, pp. 294–95; Okin, *Women in Western Political Thought*, p. 226). But this suggestion is more plausibly understood as evidence of Mill's understanding of how far patriarchy had been bred into the bones of society and thus how radical feminist reforms would have to be. Mill's insight, which is surely correct, is that to imagine the possibilities of individuality unconstrained by patriarchy, the primary bearer of patriarchal values has first to be reformed. Mill's own position on the family is, I think, much closer than Okin supposes to that articulated in her *Justice, Gender, and the Family* (New York: Basic, 1989).

26. Tulloch, pp. 159–60.

27. H. L. A. Hart, *Law, Liberty and Morality* (Oxford: Oxford University Press, 1962), p. 68.

28. See Waldron.

29. This claim might not seem to touch on the slippery slope argument that censoring pornography risks "chilling" nonpornographic expression. But it would be open to anyone to rebut the description "pornographic" by arguing successfully that the

expression in context did not eroticize inequality. Of course, some people would be deterred by the prospect of having to make such an argument. But this problem is different from the one usually associated with slippery slope arguments in this area—the problem of not being able to draw lines between classes of material. (For a discussion of such issues, see F. Schauer, "Slippery Slopes," *Harvard Law Review* 99 [1985/86]: 361–83.)

30. See, e.g., R. West, "The Feminist-Conservative Anti-Pornography Alliance and the 1986 Attorney General's Commission on Pornography Report," *American Bar Foundation Journal* (1987): 681–711.

31. See A. Rich, *The Dream of a Common Language* (New York: Norton, 1978).

3

Mill and Pornography

Robert Skipper

In a recent article in this journal,[1] David Dyzenhaus has argued that Mill, by his own principles, "must be open to the legitimacy of coercive action to eradicate pornography,"[2] that is, censorship. This conclusion, Dyzenhaus admits, is surprising. "After all, the ingredients of the principled opposition to censoring pornography appear to have their roots in *On Liberty*: in Mill's articulation of a narrow harm principle as the sole legitimate basis for state coercion; in his zeal to protect a private sphere of 'self-regarding' action for the sake of an ideal of individual autonomy or self-government; and in his defense of a right to complete freedom of expression."[3] In light of the strong prima facie case for Mill's opposition to censorship, Dyzenhaus must argue convincingly if he is to shift the consensus of Mill-inspired liberalism. I do not think that the argument is convincing enough to sway either a true Mill-inspired liberal or Mill himself.

Dyzenhaus's argument, as I understand it, runs as follows. Pornography (presumably he means not all pornography, but only that which presents "natural" acts) eroticizes the social and physical inequalities between men and women, thereby making such inequality seem both natural and sexy. Sexual domination, as one part of a much larger program of the pansocietal domination of women by men, involves an apparent willingness and an apparent complicity on the part of the dominated, and this complicity is taught, encouraged, and maintained by pornography.

These points, though never made by Mill, are in the same spirit as *The Subjection of Women*. (Mill indeed made very similar arguments against numerous discriminatory laws, institutions, and practices in his time.) Now Mill claimed in that book that the most valued right of any person in a free society is the right to autonomy, and it is precisely her autonomy that society requires each woman, as though autonomously, to choose to sacrifice. However, such a choice, Dyzenhaus continues, is a sham, because no agent can rationally choose between autonomy and subjection before experiencing both. Therefore, he concludes, whereas in his time Mill campaigned for the repeal of discriminatory laws and the abandonment of repressive customs, had Mill ever considered pornography, or were Mill alive today, he would surely recognize pornography as an important prop in an institution that is harmful to the autonomies of women. And further, he might be inclined to admit that the harm done by this institution, of which pornography is a prop, is sufficient to warrant the censorship of the prop.

I am puzzled about two points in the argument. First, given that Dyzenhaus's argument draws most of its moral force from its opposition to the evils of a social system that would indoctrinate women into being their own jailers, pornography seems to be an odd scapegoat. The wrong to be righted is that of women's being molded into "willing slaves."[4] Yet the type of pornography that Dyzenhaus speaks of is "targeted" at men, the oppressors. True, it eroticizes an institutionalized inequality between men and women, but only, or for the most part, in a way that appeals to men. Even if we grant that pornography teaches that men's domination of women is sexy, it teaches the lesson to men. Yet women, says Dyzenhaus, must cooperate for the fantasy to become real. That is, if women refuse to participate, men's fantasies stay men's fantasies, and women retain (or achieve) their autonomy. The most pernicious and disturbing aspect of inequality, according to both Dyzenhaus and Mill, is the apparent willingness of women, which both society (Mill) and pornography (Dyzenhaus) seem to expect. Women, in short, are brainwashed into thinking that they enjoy being repressed. Therefore, what would seem to be a far more obvious target for Dyzenhaus's argument is *women's literature* (that is, literature directed at women and frequently written by women), not men's pornography. Mill himself, in passages like the following, condemns the harm done by then current women authors to their female readerships. "The greater part of what women write about is mere sycophancy to men. In the case of unmarried women, much of it seems only intended to increase their chance of a husband. Many, both married and unmarried, overstep the mark, and inculcate a servility beyond what is desired or relished by any man, except the very vulgarest."[5]

The second puzzle lies in the attention that Dyzenhaus lavishes on eroticization, as though this is the only, or even the major, way of "unfairly" ensouling a false or oppressive value with passion. Dyzenhaus seems to assume that eroticizing a value is an unfair or dirty trick that bypasses reason and (hence) autonomy. But if one is to grant that this form of persuasion is unfair, one must wonder about the many other approaches that are at least as effective. Inequality can and has been romanticized, glorified, celebrated, patriotized, totemized, sacralized, proselytized, and aestheticized. Each one of these techniques involves positively associating inequality with a powerful, action-guiding emotion. Why, then, is the *eroticization* of inequality in a class by itself of tactics to be censored? Why indeed, unless the target so isolated would find few to champion it. Given the expanded harm principle that he is working with, would not Dyzenhaus have a far more interesting battle on his hands were he to consider the censorship, for example, of all literature that makes domination by men and submission by women a matter of religious conviction? Of course, such a point might prove a pretty hard sell to Mill.

As should now be clear, Dyzenhaus, in training his sights on pornography, has directed our attention to a suspiciously small, and not obviously relevant, target. But to squelch so sordid a practice as pornography by invoking so majestic a concept as Mill's harm principle is like creating a space program to dispose of waste. If the principle is powerful enough to justify censoring pornography, it must also be strong enough to restrict other things as well. For example, if Dyzenhaus's revised harm principle is strong enough to have us censor whatever encourages men's fantasies of domination, it must also, by a parity of reasoning, have us censor whatever encourages women's fantasies of subjection.

Thus, if Mill truly "must be open to the legitimacy of coercive action to eradicate pornography" he must also be open to the legitimacy of censoring women's romances, on the grounds that they glorify the delights of feminine submission. This literature (or at least some of it) is not pornography, yet such books must surely do more to perpetuate and emotionalize the myth among the victims than do men's magazines. By the same argument, Mill should also be open to the censorship of that vast body of literature and image that is directed at preparing children to assume unequal adult roles. Do not the years that Cinderella spends in resigned and unquestioned drudgery equip her perfectly for her role as wife to the prince? If Mill would use censorship "in the service of, and controlled by, the value of autonomy,"[6] then he must censor not only that literature which goads the oppressor on, but also any complementary literature which disarms the oppressed.

Surely, however, Mill would tolerate no such action. After all, it is not pornography as such that Dyzenhaus sets forth as a target of censorship, but rather pornography as one of many props for the institutionalized inequality of men and women. Were this institution to disappear, eroticized inequality would presumably sink into the background of other more or less tastelessly eroticized behaviors or objects. Dyzenhaus argues that Mill might "seriously consider" the censoring of pornography. Yet if "seriously" means more than "politely" this cannot be right. Surely Mill would not prefer the suppression of one opinion when the promotion of competing opinions is possible. For as long as there are active, constructive, and competitive approaches to counteracting the evils of any institution, no true liberal in Mill's tradition would rush headlong down the path of censorship merely out of frustrated impatience at the willful stupidity of human beings.

That there is, or ought to be, some space in human existence thus entrenched around, and sacred from authoritative intrusion, no one who professes the smallest regard to human freedom or dignity will call in question: the point to be determined is, where the limit should be placed; how large a province of human life this reserved territory should include. I apprehend that it ought to include all that part which concerns only the life, whether inward or outward, of the individual, and does not affect the interest of others, *or affects them only through the moral influence of example.*[7]

Pornography and the Cinderella story both affect the interests of others, but only through the moral influence of example; and they are thus fully within that space which Mill considers sacred from authoritative intrusion. Such remarks as this last quotation suggest that Mill would simply slam the door on feminist arguments of the sort that Dyzenhaus has presented.

As for the nature of a Millian remedy for the ill effects of pornography, one could profitably meditate on the following passage.

There is another kind of intervention which is not authoritative: when a government, instead of issuing a command and enforcing it by penalties, adopts the course so seldom resorted to by governments, and of which such important use might be made, that of giving advice, and promulgating information; or when, leaving individuals free to use their own means of pursuing any object of general interest, the government, not meddling with them, but not trusting the object solely to their care, establishes, side by side with their arrangements, an agency of its own for a like purpose. Thus, it is one thing to maintain a Church Establishment, and another to refuse toleration to other religions, or to persons professing no religion. It is one thing to provide schools or colleges, and another to require that no person shall act as an instructor of youth without a government license. There might be a national bank, or a government manufactory, without any monopoly against private banks and manufactories. There might be a post-office, without penalties against the conveyance of letters by other means. . . .[8]

Notes

I would like to thank Mark Williamson for his helpful suggestions about an earlier draft of this paper.

1. David Dyzenhaus, "John Stuart Mill and the Harm of Pornography," *Ethics* 102 (1992): 534–51.

2. Ibid., p. 550.

3. Ibid., pp. 536–37.

4. I do not wish to delve into the complexities of this paradoxical concept. Mill seemed willing enough to accept the notion, and so I shall give it to Dyzenhaus. Granted that a willing slavery is possible, granted that persons can be impressed into such a state, and granted that a willing enslavement is harmful to the slave's autonomy, Dyzenhaus (I shall argue) still cannot conclude that Mill's own principles would condone the censorship of pornography.

5. John Stuart Mill, *The Subjection of Women*, ed. Susan Moller Okin (Indianapolis: Hackett, 1988), pp. 26–27.

6. Dyzenhaus, p. 549.

7. John Stuart Mill, *Principles of Political Economy*, in *Collected Works*, vol. 3, ed. J. M. Robson (Toronto: University of Toronto Press, 1965), p. 938; the emphasis is mine.

8. Ibid., p. 937.

4

Paternalism

Gerald Dworkin

Neither one person, nor any number of persons, is warranted in saying to another human creature of ripe years, that he shall not do with his life for his own benefit what he chooses to do with it. {Mill}

I do not want to go along with a volunteer basis. I think a fellow should be compelled to become better and not let him use his discretion whether he wants to get smarter, more healthy or more honest. {General Hershey}

I take as my starting point the "one very simple principle" proclaimed by Mill *On Liberty. . .*

That principle is, that the sole end for which mankind are warranted, individually or collectively, in interfering with the liberty of action of any of their number, is self-protection. That the only purpose for which power can be rightfully exercised over any member of a civilized community, against his will, is to prevent harm to others. He cannot rightfully be compelled to do or forbear because it will be better for him to do so, because it will make him happier, because, in the opinion of others, to do so would be wise, or even right.

This principle is neither "one" nor "very simple." It is at least two principles; one asserting that self-protection or the prevention of harm to others is sometimes a sufficient warrant and the other claiming that the individual's own good is *never* a sufficient warrant for the exercise of compulsion either by the society as a whole or by its individual members. I assume that no one, with the possible exception of extreme pacifists or anarchists, questions the correctness of the first half of the principle. This essay is an examination of the negative claim embodied in Mill's principle—the objection to paternalistic interferences with a man's liberty.

I

By paternalism I shall understand roughly the interference with a person's liberty of action justified by reasons referring exclusively to the welfare, good, happiness, needs, interests or values of the person being coerced. One is always well-advised to illustrate one's definitions by examples but it is not easy to find "pure" examples of paternalistic interferences. For almost any piece of legislation is justified by several different kinds of reasons and even if historically a piece of legislation can be shown to have been introduced for purely paternalistic motives, it may be that advocates of the legislation with an antipaternalistic outlook can find sufficient reasons justifying the legislation without appealing to the reasons which were originally adduced to support it. Thus, for example, it may be that the original legislation requiring motorcyclists to wear safety helmets was introduced for purely paternalistic reasons. But the Rhode Island Supreme Court recently upheld such legislation on the grounds that it was "not persuaded that the legislature is powerless to prohibit individuals from pursuing a course of conduct which could conceivably result in their becoming public charges," thus clearly introducing reasons of a quite different kind. Now I regard this decision as being based on reasoning of a very dubious nature but it illustrates the kind of problem one has in finding examples. The following is a list of the kinds of interferences I have in mind as being paternalistic.

II

1. Laws requiring motorcyclists to wear safety helmets when operating their machines.

2. Laws forbidding persons from swimming at a public beach when lifeguards are not on duty.
3. Laws making suicide a criminal offense.
4. Laws making it illegal for women and children to work at certain types of jobs.
5. Laws regulating certain kinds of sexual conduct, for example, homosexuality among consenting adults in private.
6. Laws regulating the use of certain drugs which may have harmful consequences to the user but do not lead to anti-social conduct.
7. Laws requiring a license to engage in certain professions with those not receiving a license subject to fine or jail sentence if they do engage in the practice.
8. Laws compelling people to spend a specified fraction of their income on the purchase of retirement annuities (Social Security).
9. Laws forbidding various forms of gambling (often justified on the grounds that the poor are more likely to throw away their money on such activities than the rich who can afford to).
10. Laws regulating the maximum rates of interest for loans.
11. Laws against duelling.

In addition to laws which attach criminal or civil penalties to certain kinds of action there are laws, rules, regulations, decrees which make it either difficult or impossible for people to carry out their plans and which are also justified on paternalistic grounds. Examples of this are:

1. Laws regulating the types of contracts which will be upheld as valid by the courts, for example, (an example of Mill's to which I shall return) no man may make a valid contract for perpetual involuntary servitude.
2. Not allowing assumption of risk as a defense to an action based on the violation of a safety statute.
3. Not allowing as a defense to a charge of murder or assault the consent of the victim.

4. Requiring members of certain religious sects to have compulsory blood transfusions. This is made possible by not
   allowing the patient to have recourse to civil suits for
   assault and battery and by means of injunctions.
5. Civil commitment procedures when these are specifically
   justified on the basis of preventing the person being committed from harming himself. The D.C. Hospitalization of
   the Mentally Ill Act provides for involuntary hospitalization of a person who "is mentally ill, and because of that
   illness, is likely to injure himself or others if allowed to
   remain at liberty." The term injure in this context applies
   to unintentional as well as intentional injuries.

All of my examples are of existing restrictions on the liberty of
individuals. Obviously one can think of interferences which have
not yet been imposed. Thus one might ban the sale of cigarettes,
or require that people wear safety belts in automobiles (as
opposed to merely having them installed), enforcing this by not
allowing motorist to sue for injuries even when caused by other
drivers if the motorist was not wearing a seat belt at the time of
the accident.

I shall not be concerned with activities which though defended
on paternalistic grounds are not interferences with the liberty of
persons, for example, the giving of subsidies in kind rather than
in cash on the grounds that the recipients would not spend the
money on the goods which they really need, or not including a
$1,000 deductible provision in a basic protection automobile
insurance plan on the ground that the people who would elect it
could least afford it. Nor shall I be concerned with measures such
as "truth-in-advertising" acts and Pure Food and Drug legislation
which are often attacked as paternalistic but which should not be
considered so. In these cases all that is provided—it is true by the
use of compulsion—is information which it is presumed that
rational persons are interested in having in order to make wise
decisions. There is no interference with the liberty of the con-
sumer unless one wants to stretch a point beyond good sense and
say that his liberty to apply for a loan without knowing the true

rate of interest is diminished. It is true that sometimes there is sentiment for going further than providing information, for example when laws against usurious interest are passed preventing those who might wish to contract loans at high rates of interest from doing so, and these measures may correctly be considered paternalistic.

III

Bearing these examples in mind, let me return to a characterization of paternalism. I said earlier that I meant by the term, roughly, interference with a person's liberty for his own good. But, as some of the examples show, the class of persons whose good is involved is not always identical with the class of persons whose freedom is restricted. Thus, in the case of professional licensing it is the practitioner who is directly interfered with but it is the would-be patient whose interests are presumably being served. Not allowing the consent of the victim to be a defense to certain types of crime primarily affects the would-be aggressor but it is the interests of the willing victim that we are trying to protect. Sometimes a person may fall into both classes as would be the case if we banned the manufacture and sale of cigarettes and a given manufacturer happened to be a smoker as well.

Thus we may first divide paternalistic interferences into "pure" and "impure" cases. In "pure" paternalism the class of persons whose freedom is restricted is identical with the class of persons whose benefit is intended to be promoted by such restrictions. Examples: the making of suicide a crime, requiring passengers in automobiles to wear seat belts, requiring a Jehovah's Witness to receive a blood transfusion. In the case of "impure" paternalism in trying to protect the welfare of a class of persons we find that the only way to do so will involve restricting the freedom of other persons besides those who are benefitted. Now it might be thought that there are no cases of "impure" paternalism since any such case could always be justified on nonpaternalistic grounds, that is, in terms of preventing harm to others. Thus we might ban cigarette manufacturers from continuing to manufacture their product on the grounds that we are preventing them from causing illness to others in the same way that we prevent other manufacturers from releasing pollutants into the atmosphere, thereby causing danger to the members of the community. The difference is, however, that in the former but not the latter case the harm is of such a nature that it could be avoided by those individuals affected if they so chose. The incurring of the harm requires, so to speak, the active cooperation of the victim. It would be mistaken theoretically and hypocritical in practice to assert that our interference in such cases is just like our interference in standard cases of protecting others from harm. At the very least someone interfered with in this way can reply that no one is complaining about his activities. It may be that impure paternalism requires arguments or reasons of a stronger kind in order to be justified, since there are persons who are losing a portion of their liberty and they do not even have the solace of having it be done "in their own interest." Of course in some sense, if paternalistic justifications are ever correct, then we are protecting others, we are preventing some from injuring others, but it is important to see the differences between this and the standard case.

Paternalism then will always involve limitations on the liberty of some individuals in their own interest but it may also extend to interferences with the liberty of parties whose interests are not in question.

IV

Finally, by way of some more preliminary analysis, I want to distinguish paternalistic interference with liberty from a related type with which it is often confused. Consider, for example, legislation which forbids employees to work more than, say, forty hours per week. It is sometimes argued that such legislation is paternalistic for if employees desired such a restriction on their hours of work they could agree among themselves to impose it voluntarily. But because they do not the society imposes its own conception of their best interests upon them by the use of coercion. Hence this is paternalism.

Now it may be that some legislation of this nature is, in fact, paternalistically motivated. I am not denying that. All I want to point out is that there is another possible way of justifying such measures which is not paternalistic in nature. It is not paternalistic because, as Mill puts it in a similar context, such measures are "required not to overrule the judgment of individuals respecting their own interest, but to give effect to that judgment: they being unable to give effect to it except by concert, which concert again cannot be effectual unless it receives validity and sanction from the law." (*Principles of Political Economy*).

The line of reasoning here is a familiar one first found in Hobbes and developed with great sophistication by contemporary economists in the last decade or so. There are restrictions which are in the interests of a class of persons taken collectively but are such that the immediate interest of each individual is furthered by his violating the rule when others adhere to it. In such cases the individuals involved may need the use of compulsion to give effect to their collective judgment of their own interest by guaranteeing each individual compliance by the others. In these cases compulsion is not used to achieve some benefit which is not recognized to be a benefit by those concerned, but rather because it is the only feasible means of achieving some benefit which *is* recognized as such by all concerned. This way of viewing matters provides us with another characterization of paternalism in general. Paternalism might be thought of as the use of coercion to achieve a good which is not recognized as such by those persons for whom the good is intended. Again while this formulation captures the heart of the matter—it is surely what Mill is objecting to in *On Liberty*—the matter is not always quite like that. For example, when we force motorcyclists to wear helmets we are trying to promote a good—the protection of the person from injury—which is surely recognized by most of the individuals concerned. It is not that a cyclist doesn't value his bodily integrity; rather, as a supporter of such legislation would put it, he either places, perhaps irrationally, another value or good (freedom from wearing a helmet) above that of physical well-being or, perhaps, while recognizing the danger in the abstract, he either does not fully appreciate it or he underestimates the likelihood of its occurring. But now we are approaching the question of possible justifications of paternalistic measures and the rest of this essay will be devoted to that question.

V

I shall begin for dialectical purposes by discussing Mill's objections to paternalism and then go on to discuss more positive proposals.

An initial feature that strikes one is the absolute nature of Mill's prohibitions against paternalism. It is so unlike the carefully qualified admonitions of Mill and his fellow utilitarians on other moral issues. He speaks of self-protection as the *sole* end warranting coercion, of the individual's own goals as *never* being a sufficient warrant. Contrast this with his discussion of the prohibition against lying in *Utilitarianism*:

> Yet that even this rule, sacred as it is, admits of possible exception, is acknowledged by all moralists, the chief of which is where the with-holding of some fact . . . would save an individual . . . from great and unmerited evil.

The same tentativeness is present when he deals with justice:

> It is confessedly unjust to break faith with any one: to violate an engagement, either express or implied, or disappoint expectations raised by our own conduct, at least if we have raised these expectations knowingly and voluntarily. Like all the other obligations of justice already spoken of, this one is not regarded as absolute, but as capable of being overruled by a stronger obligation of justice on the other side.

This anomaly calls for some explanation. The structure of Mill's argument is as follows:

1. Since restraint is an evil the burden of proof is on those who propose such restraint.
2. Since the conduct which is being considered is purely self-regarding, the normal appeal to the protection of the interests of others is not available.

3. Therefore we have to consider whether reasons involving reference to the individual's own good, happiness, welfare, or interests are sufficient to overcome the burden of justification.
4. We either cannot advance the interests of the individual by compulsion, or the attempt to do so involves evils which outweigh the good done.
5. Hence the promotion of the individual's own interests does not provide a sufficient warrant for the use of compulsion.

Clearly the operative premise here is (4), and it is bolstered by claims about the status of the individual as judge and appraiser of his welfare, interests, needs, et cetera.:

With respect to his own feelings and circumstances, the most ordinary man or woman has means of knowledge immeasurably surpassing those that can be possessed by any one else.

He is the man most interested in his own well-being: the interest which any other person, except in cases of strong personal attachment, can have in it is trifling, compared to that which he himself has.

These claims are used to support the following generalizations concerning the utility of compulsion for paternalistic purposes.

The interferences of society to overrule his judgment and purposes in what only regards himself must be grounded on general presumptions; which may be altogether wrong, and even if right, are as likely as not to be missapplied to individual cases.

But the strongest of all the arguments against the interference of the public with purely personal conduct is that when it does interfere, the odds are that it interferes wrongly and in the wrong place.

All errors which the individual is likely to commit against advice and warning are far outweighed by the evil of allowing others to constrain him to what they deem his good.

Performing the utilitarian calculation by balancing the advantages and disadvantages, we find that: "Mankind are greater gainers by suffering each other to live as seems good to themselves, than by compelling each other to live as seems good to the rest." Ergo, (4).

This classical case of a utilitarian argument with all the premises spelled out is not the only line of reasoning present in Mill's discussion. There are asides, and more than asides, which look quite different and I shall deal with them later. But this is clearly the main channel of Mill's thought and it is one which has been subjected to vigorous attack from the moment it appeared—most often by fellow utilitarians. The link that they have usually seized on is, as Fitzjames Stephen put it in *Liberty, Equality, Fraternity*, the absence of proof that the "mass of adults are so well acquainted with their own interests and so much disposed to pursue them that no compulsion or restraint put upon them by any others for the purpose of promoting their interest can really promote them." Even so sympathetic a critic as H. L. A. Hart is forced to the conclusion that:

> In Chapter 5 of his essay [On Liberty] Mill carried his protests against paternalism to lengths that may now appear to us as fantastic . . . No doubt if we no longer sympathise with this criticism this is due, in part, to a general decline in the belief that individuals know their own interest best.
>
> Mill endows the average individual with "too much of the psychology of a middle-aged man whose desires are relatively fixed, not liable to be artificially stimulated by external influences; who knows what he wants and what gives him satisfaction or happiness; and who pursues these things when he can."

Now it is interesting to note that Mill himself was aware of some of the limitations on the doctrine that the individual is the best judge of his own interests. In his discussion of government intervention in general (even where the intervention does not interfere with liberty but provides alternative institutions to those of the market) after making claims which are parallel to those just discussed, for example, "People understand their own business and their own interests better, and care for them more, than the government does, or can be expected to do," he goes on to an intelligent discussion of the "very large and conspicuous exceptions" to the maxim that:

> Most persons take a juster and more intelligent view of their own interest, and of the means of promoting it than can either be prescribed to them by a general enactment of the legislature, or pointed out in the particular case by a public functionary.

Thus there are things

> of which the utility does not consist in ministering to inclinations, nor in serving the daily uses of life, and the want of which is least felt where the need is greatest. This is peculiarly true of those things which are chiefly useful as tending to raise the character of human beings. The uncultivated cannot be competent judges of cultivation. Those who most need to be made wiser and better, usually desire it least, and, if they desire it, would be incapable of finding the way to it by their own lights.
>
> . . . A second exception to the doctrine that individuals are the best judges of their own interest, is when an individual attempts to decide irrevocably now what will be best for his interest at some future and distant time. The presumption in favor of individual judgment is only legitimate, where the judgment is grounded on actual, and especially on present, personal experience; not where it is formed antecedently to experience, and not suffered to be reversed even after experience has condemned it.

The upshot of these exceptions is that Mill does not declare that there should never be government interference with the economy but rather that

> . . . in every instance, the burden of making out a strong case should be thrown not on those who resist but those who recommend government interference. Letting alone, in short, should be the general practice: every departure from it, unless required by some great good, is a certain evil.

In short, we get a presumption, not an absolute prohibition. The question is why doesn't the argument against paternalism go the same way?

I suggest that the answer lies in seeing that in addition to a purely utilitarian argument Mill uses another as well. As a utilitarian, Mill has to show, in Fitzjames Stephen's words, that: "Self-protection apart, no good object can be attained by any compulsion which is not in itself a greater evil than the absence of the object which the compulsion obtains." To show this is impossible, one reason being that it isn't true. Preventing a man from selling himself into slavery (a paternalistic measure which Mill himself accepts as legitimate), or from taking heroin, or from driving a car without wearing seat belts may constitute a lesser evil than allowing him to do any of these things. A consistent utilitarian can only argue against paternalism on the grounds that it (as a matter of fact) does not maximize the good. It is always a contingent question that may be refuted by the evidence. But there is also a non-contingent argument which runs through *On Liberty*. When Mill states that "there is a part of the life of every person who has come to years of discretion, within which the individuality of that person ought to reign uncontrolled either by any other person or by the public collectively," he is saying something about what it means to be a person, an autonomous agent. It is because coercing a person for his own good denies this status as an independent entity that Mill objects to it so strongly and in such absolute terms. To be able to choose is a good that is independent of the wisdom of what is chosen. A man's "mode of laying out his existence is the best, not because it is the best in itself, but because it is his own mode.... It is the privilege and proper condition of a human being, arrived at the maturity of his faculties, to use and interpret experience in his own way."

As further evidence of this line of reasoning in Mill, consider the one exception to his prohibition against paternalism.

> In this and most civilised countries, for example, an engagement by which a person should sell himself, or allow himself to be sold, as a slave, would be null and void; neither enforced by law nor by opinion. The ground for thus limiting his power of voluntarily disposing of his own lot in life, is apparent, and is very clearly seen in this extreme case. The reason for not interfering, unless for the sake of others, with a person's voluntary acts, is consideration

for his liberty. His voluntary choice is evidence that what he so chooses is desirable, or at least endurable, to him, and his good is on the whole best provided for by allowing him to take his own means of pursuing it. But by selling himself for a slave, he abdicates his liberty; he foregoes any future use of it beyond that single act. He therefore defeats, in his own case, the very purpose which is the justification of allowing him to dispose of himself. He is no longer free; but is thenceforth in a position which has no longer the presumption in its favour, that would be afforded by his voluntarily remaining in it. The principle of freedom cannot require that he should be free not to be free. It is not freedom to be allowed to alienate his freedom.

Now leaving aside the fudging on the meaning of freedom in the last line, it is clear that part of this argument is incorrect. While it is true that *future* choices of the slave are not reasons for thinking that what he chooses then is desirable for him, what is at issue is limiting his immediate choice; and since this choice is made freely, the individual may be correct in thinking that his interests are best provided for by entering such a contract. But the main consideration for not allowing such a contract is the need to preserve the liberty of the person to make future choices. This gives us a principle—a very narrow one—by which to justify some paternalistic interferences. Paternalism is justified only to preserve a wider range of freedom for the individual in question. How far this principle could be extended, whether it can justify all the cases in which we are inclined upon reflection to think paternalistic measures justified, remains to be discussed. What I have tried to show so far is that there are two strains of argument in Mill—one a straight-forward utilitarian mode of reasoning and one which relies not on the goods which free choice leads to but on the absolute value of the choice itself. The first cannot establish any absolute prohibition but at most a presumption and indeed a fairly weak one given some fairly plausible assumptions about human psychology; the second, while a stronger line of argument, seems to me to allow on its own grounds a wider range of paternalism than might be suspected. I turn now to a consideration of these matters.

VI

We might begin looking for principles governing the acceptable use of paternalistic power in cases where it is generally agreed that it is legitimate. Even Mill intends his principles to be applicable only to mature individuals, not those in what he calls "non-age." What is it that justifies us in interfering with children? The fact that they lack some of the emotional and cognitive capacities required in order to make fully rational decisions. It is an empirical question to just what extent children have an adequate conception of their own present and future interests but there is not much doubt that there are many deficiencies. For example, it is very difficult for a child to defer gratification for any considerable period of time. Given these deficiencies and given the very real and permanent dangers that may befall the child, it becomes not only permissible but even a duty of the parent to restrict the child's freedom in various ways. There is however an important moral limitation on the exercise of such parental power which is provided by the notion of the child eventually coming to see the correctness of his parent's interventions. Parental paternalism may be thought of as a wager by the parent on the child's subsequent recognition of the wisdom of the restrictions. There is an emphasis on what could be called future-oriented consent—on what the child will come to welcome, rather than on what he does welcome.

The essence of this idea has been incorporated by idealist philosophers into various types of "real-will" theory as applied to fully adult persons. Extensions of paternalism are argued for by claiming that in various respects, chronologically mature individuals share the same deficiencies in knowledge, capacity to think rationally, and the ability to carry out decisions that children possess. Hence in interfering with such people we are in effect doing what they would do if they were fully rational. Hence we are not really opposing their will, hence we are not really interfering with their freedom. The dangers of this move have been sufficiently exposed by Berlin in his Two Concepts of Liberty. I see no gain in theoretical clarity nor in practical advantage in trying to pass over the real nature of the interferences with liberty that we impose on others. Still the basic notion of consent is important and seems to me the only acceptable way of trying to delimit an area of justified paternalism.

Let me start by considering a case where the consent is not hypothetical in nature. Under certain conditions it is rational for an individual to agree that others should force him to act in ways which, at the time of action, the individual may not see as desirable. If, for example, a man knows that he is subject to breaking his resolves when temptation is present, he may ask a friend to refuse to entertain his requests at some later stage.

A classical example is given in the Odyssey when Odysseus commands his men to tie him to the mast and refuse all future orders to be set free, because he knows the power of the Sirens to enchant men with their songs. Here we are on relatively sound ground in later refusing Odysseus' request to be set free. He may even claim to have changed his mind but, since it is *just* such changes that he wished to guard against, we are entitled to ignore them.

A process analogous to this may take place on a social rather than individual basis. An electorate may mandate its representatives to pass legislation which when it comes time to "pay the price" may be unpalatable. I may believe that a tax increase is necessary to halt inflation though I may resent the lower pay check each month. However in both this case and that of Odysseus, the measure to be enforced is specifically requested by the party involved and at some point in time there is genuine consent and agreement on the part of those persons whose liberty is infringed. Such is not the case for the paternalistic measures we have been speaking about. What must be involved here is not consent to specific measures but rather consent to a system of government, run by elected representatives, with an understanding that they may act to safeguard our interests in certain limited ways.

I suggest that since we are all aware of our irrational propensities, deficiencies in cognitive and emotional capacities, and avoidable and unavoidable ignorance, it is rational and prudent for us to in effect take out "social insurance policies." We may argue for and against proposed paternalistic measures in terms of what fully rational individuals would accept as forms of protection. Now clearly, since the initial agreement is not about specific measures we are dealing with a more-or-less blank check and therefore there have to be carefully defined limits. What I am looking for are certain kinds of conditions which make it plausible to suppose that rational people could reach agreement to limit their liberty even when others' interests are not affected.

Of course as in any kind of agreement schema there are great difficulties in deciding what rational individuals would or would not accept. Particularly in sensitive areas of personal liberty, there is always a danger of the dispute over agreement and rationality being a disguised version of evaluative and normative disagreement.

Let me suggest types of situations in which it seems plausible to suppose that fully rational individuals would agree to having paternalistic restrictions imposed upon them. It is reasonable to suppose that there are "goods" such as health which any person would want to have in order to pursue his own good—no matter how that good is conceived. This is an argument used in connection with compulsory education for children but it seems to me that it can be extended to other goods which have this character. Then one could agree that the attainment of such goods should be promoted even when not recognized to be such, at the moment, by the individuals concerned.

An immediate difficulty arises from the fact that people are always faced with competing goods and that there may be reasons why even a value such as health—or indeed life—may be overridden by competing values. Thus the problem with the Jehovah's Witness and blood transfusions. It may be more important for him to reject "impure substances" than to go on living. The difficult problem that must be faced is whether one can give sense to the notion of a person irrationally attaching weights to competing values.

Consider a person who knows the statistical data on the probability of being injured when not wearing seat belts in an automobile and knows the types and gravity of the various injuries. He also insists that the inconvenience attached to fastening the belt every time he gets in and out of the car outweighs for him the possible risks to himself. I am inclined in this case to think that such a weighing is irrational. Given his life plans, which we are assuming are those of the average person, his interests and commitments already undertaken, I think it is safe to predict that we can find inconsistencies in his calculations at some point. I am assuming that this is not a man who for some conscious or unconscious reasons is trying to injure himself nor is he a man who just likes to "live dangerously." I am assuming that he is like us in all the relevant respects but just puts an enormously high negative value on inconvenience—one which does not seem comprehensible or reasonable.

It is always possible, of course, to assimilate this person to creatures like myself. I, also, neglect to fasten my seat belt and I concede such behavior is not rational but not because I weigh the inconvenience differently from those who fasten the belts. It is just that having made (roughly) the same calculation as everybody else, I ignore it in my actions. [Note: a much better case of weakness of the will than those usually given in ethics tests.] A plausible explanation for this deplorable habit is that although I know in some intellectual sense what the probabilities and risks are I do not fully appreciate them in an emotionally genuine manner.

We have two distinct types of situation in which a man acts in a nonrational fashion. In one case he attaches incorrect weights to some of his values; in the other he neglects to act in accordance with his actual preferences and desires. Clearly there is a stronger and more persuasive argument for paternalism in the latter situation. Here we are really not—by assumption—imposing a good on another person. But why may we not extend our interference to what we might call evaluative delusions? After all, in the case of cognitive delusions we are prepared, often, to act against the expressed will of the person involved. If a man believes that when he jumps out the window he will float upwards—Robert Nozick's example—would not we detain him, forcibly if necessary? The reply will be that this man doesn't wish to be injured and if we could convince him that he is mistaken as to the consequences of his action, he would not wish to perform the action. But part of what is involved in claiming that the man who doesn't fasten his seat-belts is attaching an incorrect weight to the inconvenience of fastening them is that if he were to be involved in an accident and severely injured he would look back and admit that the inconvenience wasn't as bad as all that. So there is a sense in which, if I could convince him of the consequences of his action, he also would not wish to continue his present course of action. Now the notion of consequences being used here is covering a lot of ground. In one case it's being used to indicate what will or can happen as a result of a course of action and in the other it's making a prediction about the future evaluation of the consequences—in the first sense—of a course of action. And whatever the difference between facts and values—whether it be hard and fast or soft and slow—we are genuinely more reluctant to consent to interferences where evaluative differences are the issue. Let me now consider another factor which comes into play in some of these situations which may make an important difference in our willingness to consent to paternalistic restrictions.

Some of the decisions we make are of such a character that they produce changes which are in one or another way irreversible. Situations are created in which it is difficult or impossible to return to anything like the initial stage at which the decision was made. In particular, some of these changes will make it impossible to continue to make reasoned choices in the future. I am thinking specifically of decisions which involve taking drugs that are physically or psychologically addictive and those which are destructive of one's mental and physical capacities.

I suggest we think of the imposition of paternalistic interferences in situations of this kind as being a kind of insurance policy which we take out against making decisions which are far-reaching, potentially dangerous and irreversible. Each of these factors is important. Clearly there are many decisions we make that are relatively irreversible. In deciding to learn to play chess, I could predict in view of my general interest in games that some portion of my free time was going to be preempted and that it would not be easy to give up the game once I acquired a certain competence. But my whole life style was not going to be jeopardized in an extreme manner. Further it might be argued that even with addictive drugs such as heroin one's normal life plans would not be seriously interfered with if an inexpensive and adequate supply were readily available. So this type of argument might have a much narrower scope than appears to be the case at first.

A second class of cases concerns decisions which are made under extreme psychological and sociological pressures. I am not thinking here of the making of the decision as being something one is pressured into—for example, a good reason for making duelling illegal is that unless this is done many people might have to manifest their courage and integrity in ways in which they would rather not do so—but rather of decisions, such as that to commit suicide, which are usually made at a point where the individual is not thinking clearly and calmly about the nature of his decision. In addition, of course, this comes under the previous heading of all-too-irrevocable decisions. Now there are practical steps which a society could take if it wanted to decrease the possibility of suicide—for example not paying social security benefits to the survivors or, as religious institutions do, not allowing persons to be buried with the same status as natural deaths. I think we may count these as interferences with the liberty of persons to attempt suicide and the question is whether they are justifiable.

Using my argument schema the question is whether rational individuals would consent to such limitations. I see no reason for them to consent to an absolute prohibition but I do think it is reasonable for them to agree to some kind of enforced waiting period. Since we are all aware of the possibility of temporary states, such as great fear or depression, that are inimical to the making of well-informed and rational decisions, it would be prudent for all of us if there were some kind of institutional arrangement whereby we were restrained from making a decision which is so irreversible. What this would be like in practice is difficult to envisage and it may be that if no practical arrangements were feasible we would have to conclude that there should be no restriction at all on this kind of action. But we might have a "cooling off" period, in much the same way that we now require couples who file for divorce to go through a waiting period. Or, more far-fetched, we might imagine a Suicide Board composed of a psychologist and another member picked by the applicant. The Board would be required to meet and talk with the person proposing to take his life, though its approval would not be required.

A third class of decisions—these classes are not supposed to be disjoint—involves dangers which are either not sufficiently understood or appreciated correctly by the persons involved. Let me illustrate, using the example of cigarette smoking, a number of possible cases.

1. A person may not know the facts—for example, smoking between one and two packs a day shortens life expectancy 6.2 years, the costs and pain of the illness caused by smoking, et cetera.
2. A person may know the facts, wish to stop smoking, but not have the requisite will-power.
3. A person may know the facts but not have them play the correct role in her calculation because, say, she discounts the danger psychologically since it is remote in time and/or inflates the attractiveness of other consequences of the decisions.

In case 1 what is called for is education, the posting of warnings, et cetera. In case 2 there is no theoretical problem. We are not imposing a good on someone who rejects it. We are simply using coercion to enable people to carry out their own goals. (Note: There obviously is a difficulty in that only a subclass of the individuals affected wish to be prevented from doing what they are doing.) In case 3 there is a sense in which we are imposing a good on someone in that given their current appraisal of the facts they do wish to be restricted. But in another sense we are not imposing a good since what is being claimed—and what must be shown or at least argued for—is that an accurate accounting would lead them to reject the current course of action. Now we all know that such cases exist, that we are prone to disregarding dangers that are only possibilities, that immediate pleasures are often magnified and distorted.

If in addition the dangers are severe and far-reaching, we could agree to allow the state a certain degree of power to intervene in such situations. The difficulty is in specifying in advance, even vaguely, the class of cases in which intervention will be legitimate.

A related difficulty is that of drawing a line so that it is not the case that all ultra-hazardous activities are ruled out, for example, mountain-climbing, bull-fighting, sports-car racing, et cetera. There are some risks—even very great ones—which a person is entitled to take with his life.

A good deal depends on the nature of the deprivation—for example, does it prevent the person from engaging in the activity completely or merely limit his participation—and how important to the nature of the activity is the absence of restriction when this is weighed against the role that the activity plays in the life of the person. In the case of automobile seat belts, for example, the restriction is trivial in nature, interferes not at all with the use or enjoyment of the activity, and does, I am assuming, considerably reduce a high risk of serious injury. Whereas, for example, making mountain-climbing illegal completely prevents a person from engaging in an activity which may play an important role in his life and his conception of the person he is.

In general, the easiest cases to handle are those which can be argued about in the terms which Mill thought to be so important—a concern not just for the happiness or welfare, in some broad sense, of the individual but rather a concern for the autonomy and freedom of the person. I suggest that we would be most likely to consent to paternalism in those instances in which it preserves and enhances for the individual his ability to rationally consider and carry out his own decisions.

I have suggested in this essay a number of types of situations in which it seems plausible that rational men would agree to granting the legislative powers of a society the right to impose restrictions on what Mill calls "self-regarding" conduct. However, rational men knowing something about the resources of ignorance, ill-will and stupidity available to the lawmakers of a society—a good case in point is the history of drug legislation in the United States—will be concerned to limit such intervention to a minimum. I suggest in closing two principles designed to achieve this end.

In all cases of paternalistic legislation there must be a heavy and clear burden of proof placed on the authorities to demonstrate the exact nature of the harmful effects (or beneficial consequences) to be avoided (or achieved) and the probability of their occurrence. The burden of proof here is twofold—what lawyers distinguish as the burden of going forward and the burden of persuasion. That the authorities have the burden of going forward means that it is up to them to raise the question and bring forward evidence of the evils to be avoided. Unlike the case of new drugs, where the manufacturer must produce some evidence that the drug has been tested and found not harmful, no citizen has to show with respect to self-regarding conduct that it is not harmful or promotes his best interest. In addition the nature and cogency of the evidence for the harmfulness of the course of action must be set at a high level. To paraphrase a formulation of the burden of proof for criminal proceedings—better ten men ruin themselves than one man be unjustly deprived of liberty.

Finally, I suggest a principle of the least restrictive alternative. If there is an alternative way of accomplishing the desired end without restricting liberty, then although it may involve great expense, inconvenience, et cetera, the society must adopt it.

5

Paternalism, Utility, and Fairness

Richard J. Arneson

Liberals of various philosophical persuasions, perhaps including John Locke and J. S. Mill, have espoused a familiar principle that I will call the *liberty principle*, which holds that people should be left free to do whatever they choose unless their conduct threatens harm (in specified ways) to nonconsenting others. One implication of the liberty principle is *anti-paternalism*: restriction of a person's liberty to carry out a voluntarily chosen course of conduct should never be imposed for the purpose of benefitting either that person herself or others who voluntarily consent to be affected by that conduct.[1] Another implication is *no enforced charity*: if a person's conduct threatens no harm to nonconsenting others, restricting his liberty to carry out that conduct in order to force him to act for the benefit of others is never justified.[2] In *On Liberty* Mill attempted to develop a utilitarian argument for the liberty principle but critics have insisted that either the argument, if it is genuinely utilitarian, doesn't work, or if it does work, then it isn't genuinely utilitarian.[3]

In this paper I accept for the sake of argument the truth of all the empirically doubtful premises that Mill assembles to make his utilitarian case for the liberty principle, and I assume further that the logic of the arguments that Mill constructs with these premises is impeccable. My worry is that Mill's arguments even if successful in their own terms may be objectionable on grounds of fairness. Mill's arguments for the liberty principle appealing to the values of individuality and autonomy have an ideological thrust insofar as they ignore altogether the predictable distributive effects on more and less able agents of the operation of his proposed rules of "no paternalism" and "no enforced charity". Once noted, the point is obvious with respect to the "no enforced charity" component of the liberty principle, so my argument concentrates on Mill's grounds for the rejection of paternalism.

Joel Feinberg has recently produced a nonutilitarian defense of the antipaternalism component of the liberty principle that is noteworthy for its sophisticated account of the concept of voluntary choice and for its spirited defense of a principle of personal sovereignty seen as underlying an antipaternalist policy.[4] I show that Feinberg's account of voluntary choice provokes its own fairness objection against antipaternalism and that his appeal to personal sovereignty is just as problematic as Mill's utilitarianism.

1. Mill's Argument

The unfeasibility of perfect screening

Mill writes, "But the strongest of all the arguments against the interference of the public with purely personal conduct, is that when it does interfere, the odds are that it interferes wrongly, and in the wrong place."[5] This comment signals the level of abstraction at which Mill's argument is pitched. We are considering a rule regarding the treatment of paternalistic proposals that is to guide a policymaking public authority that must make decisions with limited and imperfect information about the impact the policies it is considering would have on the welfare of individual citizens. Moreover, the cost of tailoring a policy of interference to the individual case would be prohibitive even if perfect information were available. Any feasible policy must make broad rough classifications. We seek what is in effect a constitutional rule to guide policymaking in the nonideal world.

Consider a stylized description of a paternalistic decision. The public authority is deliberating about whether to prohibit a type of conduct that all agree harms no one except the agents themselves and others who freely consent to bear its consequences. Mill claims that for all proposed paternalistic restrictions, the loss to those hurt by the restriction outweighs the benefit to those helped by it. Regarding this claim, critics chide Mill for lapsing into uncharacteristically dogmatic judgment on empirical issues about which a utilitarian should be openminded. Let us give Mill the benefit of the doubt by assuming at least provisionally that his claim turns out true. What then?

In practice, paternalistic restrictions will constrain the liberty of some who would be better off in the absence of the restriction and of some who would be better off if the restriction is imposed. To some extent sheer luck determines who gains and who loses from paternalism, but we can abstract from this factor by concentrating on the expected gain or loss in welfare that an individual faces from a given proposed paternalistic restriction. Such restrictions override the judgment of the individual concerning what is best for herself. The better one's own judgment in these matters, the greater the chance that the paternalistic restriction will have bad consequences in its application to one's own case. The "traditions and customs of other people", Mill writes, should not be a law to the individual, because "their experience may be too narrow; or they may not have interpreted it rightly", or "their interpretation of experience may be correct, but unsuitable to him", or again, to conform to custom "merely *as* custom" does not develop the individual's powers of practical judgment (p. 262). Individuals obviously differ markedly from one another in their abilities reasonably to decide whether they will be better off following or flouting commonsense maxims of prudence. The deliberative abilities required for practical judgment involve choice of goals as well as choice of means. Individuals also differ widely in their capacities to make good any of their decision-making defects, when plans go awry, by their perseverance and grit, shrewd and creative improvisation, and so on. Overall we know that if we were to rank individuals according to their self-regarding virtues, their composite scores would range all the way from "wise" to "foolish" and from "competent" to "incompetent".

Mill surmises that adhering to a policy of no paternalism will stimulate the development of people's skills at rational deliberation regarding their ends and of the character traits that will best enable them to achieve their ends. He may be right about this. Still, people differ widely in their native capacities for deliberation about plans and skillful execution of them. So the combination of the good effect of stimulating one's capacities and the bad effect of letting one's present incapacities express themselves in action will affect people's prospects of welfare in different ways, depending on their achieved and potential levels of self-regarding virtue and other particulars of their situation.

The Fairness Objection

To reiterate, Mill's claim is that every feasible paternalistic social rule would lower welfare on balance. This utilitarian case for strict antipaternalism could be correct yet have disturbing implications for the distribution of welfare. A ban on paternalism in effect gives to the haves and takes from the have-nots. Left unrestrained in self-regarding matters, more able agents are more likely to do better for themselves choosing among an unrestricted range of options, whereas less able agents are more likely to opt for a bad option that paternalism would have removed from the choice set. In Mill's utilitarian calculation, it turns out that under a no-paternalism rule the losses, if any, suffered by the less able (whom we suppose are on average worse off to begin with) are outweighed by gains enjoyed by the more able (whom we suppose are on average better off to begin with).[6]

No doubt in Mill's most optimistic scenario, everybody gains under no paternalism. But to give much credence to this possibility requires us to take the more fanciful flights of Mill's rhetoric very seriously indeed. One of the more puzzling features of Mill's argument is his fixation of attention on the most wonderful possibilities of human development that might unfold if society scrupulously refrained from coercive interference with liberty in self-regarding matters. The serious worries about antipaternalism become apparent only in exploring worst-case scenarios and the likelihood they will befall at least some unfortunate persons. Leaving aside the completely unsupported conjecture that everybody gains by strict antipaternalism, we may worry that for all but the most hardboiled utilitarians, a policy that maximizes utility by making the worse off even worse off than they otherwise would be is unacceptable.

Here we touch one strand of the many and various justice-based objections to utilitarianism. Utilitarianism is distribution-insensitive: the distribution of utility across persons makes no difference whatsoever to utilitarian judgment of actions and policies except insofar as implementing one or another distribution of utility causally affects the total amount of utility in the long run. The insensitivity of utilitarianism to distributional concerns encompasses several distinct criticisms, one being that utilitarianism goes wrong in regarding only aggregate totals or averages of welfare while ignoring altogether the value of equal distribution of welfare among persons. The principle of equality of welfare holds that other things equal it is morally bad that social arrangements leave some people worse off than others. As stated, the principle is vague in not specifying how to weight the values of more welfare against more equality of welfare and against other independant moral concerns when there is conflict among them. Maximin, Nicholas Rescher's effective average, and Paul Weirich's weighted utilitarianism are rules that offer alternative ways of resolving one aspect of this conflict, by proposing alternative rules of trade-off between the norms of "Maximize welfare!" and "See to it that welfare is equally distributed!"[7] (Weirich's suggested rule holds that the moral value of a gain of welfare varies directly with its size and inversely with the final relative welfare position of the person who gains. For a marginal gain of welfare, the rule holds that the value of the gain is inversely proportional to the initial relative welfare position of the person who gains. In other words, the worse off a person is in terms of welfare, the better it is, from a moral standpoint, to secure a gain of welfare for that person). On any of these distribution-sensitive alternatives to utilitarianism, which value equality of welfare for its own sake,[8] it could be the case that even if a strict prohibition on paternalism should turn out to be welfare-maximizing, considerations of distributive fairness would recommend the enactment of some paternalist rules. Paternalism might then prove morally acceptable even if arguendo we concede to Mill all of the empirically controversial assumptions that he uses to build his case for an absolute no-paternalism rule. Mill's brand of utilitarian libertarianism, even if genuinely utilitarian, might be vulnerable to objections of fairness. Indeed, given the specific character of the arguments that Mill makes, a stronger conclusion is warranted: Mill's arguments for strict antipaternalism, to the extent they are accepted, simultaneously show that this antipaternalism is justified on straight utilitarian grounds and that it is unjustifiable on weighted utilitarian grounds that balance utility against equality.

Succeeding subsections will defend this preliminary conclusion against further arguments that are either raised by Mill or that might plausibly be urged on his behalf.

Effects on Third Parties: Mill on Progress

In the foregoing discussion the implicit assumption has been that in considering whether a paternalistic proposal is acceptable we are entitled to reckon only gains and losses to the persons whom we propose to restrict and to assume that the effects of restriction on third parties (parties not consenting to the transaction) will be nonsignificant. Mill emphatically does not make this assumption, so we need to see what happens to the argument when it is dropped. Mill observes that where something other than the individual's own character is the rule of conduct, "there is wanting one of the principal ingredients of human happiness, and quite the chief ingredient of individual and social progress" (p. 261). One of the sources of social progress that Mill has in mind is that in a society that eschews paternalism individuals will engage in a wide variety of "experiments of living" and will learn from the successes and failures of the other people's experiments. Nonpaternalism is the antidote to Chinese stationariness (pp. 273–274). In the short run people can adapt their life plans in order to take into account lessons learned from the experiences of others, and in the long run individual judgment selects the best from each generation's crop of experiments in living, so over time there is progress in individual culture. Whether my life plan succeeds or fails, my open engagement in it benefits others either through the cautionary lessons it imparts or as a model worthy of emulation. Refraining from paternalistic interference with my life has spillover benefits for those who would learn from it. As Mill puts it, "the worth of different modes of life should be proved practically, when any one thinks fit to try them" (p. 261).

Mill lays heavy stress on one possible case of progress by way of free experimentation: the less able agents benefit by observing the creative innovations exhibited by the realized life plans of the most able. He writes: "The initiation of all wise or noble things, comes and must come from individuals; generally at first from some one individual. The honour and glory of the average man is that he is capable of following that initiative; that he can respond internally to wise and noble things, and be led to them with his eyes open" (p. 269)

More generally, all people in society benefit in uncontroversial ways over the long run by the increases in material progress that are stimulated by innovations produced by persons of genius that would not have come about if the geniuses had not been free to go their own way unhampered by paternalistic restrictions. Since the geniuses who will contribute to material progress cannot be identified in advance of their contributions, in order to give free space to them one must give free space to all persons. Rising material progress is a predictable byproduct of refraining from paternalistic interference.

It should be evident that the fairness worries about Mill's antipaternalism are not allayed by this optimistic invocation of social progress. As before, I will not challenge the factual assertions that Mill makes, but simply check to see if they carry the argument as he imagines. The appeal to these spillover benefits of free experiment does not of course rule out a straight utilitarian justification of some paternalistic rules, because it might be the case that almost all the benefits of free experimentation are generated by permitting individuals broad but not unlimited freedom to carry out their life plans without suffering paternalistic

interference. Mill himself mentions the possibility that a paternalist policy could be limited to blocking individuals from following a very small number of life plans universally condemned
by experience (p. 281). For example, a government might generally permit the consumption of dangerous recreational drugs
while banning the use of a few drugs that are reliably deemed to
be extremely harmful and to offer extremely unfavorable short-
term pleasure to long-term deterioration ratios. Sidestepping this
issue of the bearing of spillover benefits on the adequacy of Mill's
utilitarian argument, I want to determine whether these benefits
might mitigate the fairness objection to Mill's strict antipaternalism. Any mitigating appearance is due to myopic concentration on just one of the several cases that need to be considered.

We need to consider socially valuable learning in the short run
(affecting the present generation) and in the long run (affecting
future generations) from successful and unsuccessful experiments
in living carried out by more and less able agents. The learners in
question who benefit from the experiments of others can of course
be either more or less able. Moreover, it is obvious that mislearning
also occurs, as when publicity about the stimulus to creative artists
provided by selective drug usage prompts others to imitate their
example, to their detriment.

A complication about the definition of "paternalism" arises
here. If in the light of cases like that just mentioned we restrict
the liberty of experimenters in order to protect the welfare of
those who are unduly likely to draw incorrect lessons for their
own lives from the experiments, is such restriction paternalistic?
The answer is "Yes" insofar as the restriction counts as a restriction of the liberty of the potential mislearners; the restriction
would then be an instance of what Gerald Dworkin calls
"impure" paternalism, in which the class of persons whose liberty
is restricted is not identical with the class of persons for the sake
of whom the restriction is imposed.[9]

However this definitional point is decided, the possibility of
mislearning alerts us to a more general phenomenon, namely
that more and less able agents have significantly different capacities to gather and correctly to interpret information generated

by other people's experiments in living. Also, agents vary in their capacities to integrate the insights so gained into their own self-regarding decisionmaking. The benefits and costs of learning from free experimentation in the ways that Mill extolls will in many cases fall unevenly on more and less able individuals. Once again it appears likely on Mill's own assumptions that a strict ban on paternalistic restriction of liberty will in some of its applications benefit the better off at the expense of the worse off, and so be unfair even if utility-maximizing.

Appeals to the benefits to society from unsuccessful experiments in living and to the benefits to future generations to be gleaned from the experience of the free experiments of the present generation also raise worrisome fairness issues. Take the second appeal first. Mill views with Victorian optimism the long-run welfare prospects of a regime of strict antipaternalism. Imagine he is right about this. Strict antipaternalism might then be justified by utilitarian calculation even if this policy guide is disadvantageous for the members of the present generation, provided that their losses are offset by gains to future members of society. But this use of the present generation as cannon fodder for the future is morally problematic, particularly so on the assumption that with social progress the average welfare level will rise with each succeeding generation. Again Mill is proposing a taking from the worse off to advantage the already better off. At some trade-off ratio this might be acceptable policy, but straight utilitarianism gives no weight at all to equality of welfare and thus countenances sacrifices of present persons for the sake of future persons that many will regard as unfair.

A similar point holds for beneficial social learning from the egregrious imprudence of the less able agents. The "unblinking accountant's eye"[10] of the utilitarian registers equally the loss suffered by the less able agent who stumbles in the gutter in a laissez-faire regime and the subsequent gain accruing to more able agents who shrewdly learn from this mishap how to avoid similar stumbles. But according to welfare egalitarianism adherence to antipaternalism in such cases amounts to unfairly using one person as a mere means to the benefit of others.

Mill's discussion of spillover benefits is polemically slanted insofar as it highlights harmonious, rosy possibilities and ignores equally likely but more troublesome cases which pose acute conflicts of distribution.

Strong and Weak Paternalism

A plausible objection to my argument to this point is that Mill is at most (depending on what one makes of his discussion of voluntary slavery contracts[11]) unequivocally opposed only to strong paternalism, that is, paternalistic restriction that involves an overriding of the restricted person's own judgment of the ultimate goals he aims to fulfill by his action. The claim then is that Mill is not opposed to weak paternalism, that is, to restriction involving an overriding only of the restricted person's own judgment of the means that are best suited to advance his chosen goals. But the worry that Mill's antipaternalism might be unfair to less able agents dissolves—or so the argument goes—once it is understood that the scope of his antipaternalism is limited to the strong variety.

I have two responses by way of rebuttal: (1) the textual basis for interpreting Mill as a weak paternalist is shaky, and (2) in any event there are cases where the welfare egalitarian argument for strong paternalism would be persuasive against Mill, if Mill were indeed a clear-cut opponent of strong paternalism.

Mill discusses acting on a mistaken belief about the means needed to achieve one's goals when he sketches the example of forcibly detaining someone who is about to venture unawares onto an unsafe bridge. The ground of interference is the reasonable presumption that the person is unaware of the rickety condition of the bridge. Once the individual is apprised of the true condition of the bridge, "when there is not a certainty, but only a danger of mischief, no one but the person himself can judge of the sufficiency of the motive which may prompt him to incur the risk" (p. 294). This passage is puzzling. If we trust the person's prudential judgment, why not presume he can correctly decide whether the gain to himself from venturing on the bridge is worth the certain loss to himself from its collapse? (He may be bent on suicide and not inclined to explain this intention to would-be do-gooders like us). If we do not trust the person's judgment, why presume that even with correct information the person can reasonably factor the risky or uncertain prospect of venturing on the bridge into his prudential decisionmaking?[12] If our ignorance of the person's goals precludes anything beyond temporary detention for the purpose of conveying relevant information when there is a chance the bridge may collapse, why doesn't this same ignorance preclude sustained interference when the collapse of the bridge is a certainty? The principle suggested by Mill's treatment of the example is not tolerance of weak paternalism and only weak paternalism, rather something like "Paternalistic restriction of a person's liberty is always wrong unless it is done either (a) to prevent the person's certain death or (b) as a temporary expedient in order to supply information that appears to be importantly relevant to the person's choice and of which he appears to be ignorant."[13] Except perhaps with regard to immediately life-threatening situations, Mill does not seem ready to countenance paternalistic restriction that is needed to counteract the decisionmaking disabilities of less able agents. As Mill elsewhere remarks, "If a person possesses any tolerable amount of common sense and experience, his own mode of laying out his existence is the best, not because it is the best in itself, but because it is his own mode" (p. 270). One's own mode of laying out one's life includes choice of means as well as choice of ultimate goals, and the precondition of one's own mode being best is not that it is particularly well-chosen, much less that it could not be improved upon by intelligent interference, but rather that one has a "tolerable" level of decisionmaking talent—which in view of the unsafe bridge passage I would interpret minimally as the requirement that the agent be neither feebleminded nor insane.

The welfare egalitarian fairness argument justifies some strong paternalism. In extreme cases the decisionmaking processes of less able agents that shape their fundamental personal values and goals may be defective to the point that coercive interference with their self-regarding choices may be justified as part of a process whereby individuals are encouraged to rethink their goals with fuller deliberative rationality. In such extreme cases strong paternalism can foster individuality, the value that Mill considers a prime ingredient and determiner of an individual's happiness. The problem for the weak paternalist position is that it concedes too much ground to the opposition. Suppose that factual ignorance, errors in deductive reasoning, failure of uptake from statistical data, framing errors, the basing of choice on nonevidential cognitive dissonance reinforcement, and the like[14] can sufficiently distort a person's judgment as to how best to achieve his ends to warrant paternalistic interference—as the weak paternalist admits. Why then don't the same irrational proclivities, operating through the processes that determine people's basic preferences, sometimes warrant strong paternalistic interference—even though the weak paternalist must on principle deny this possibility? Moreover, the same distributive fairness worries that bolster the argument for acceptance of weak paternalism will bolster the argument for acceptance of strong paternalism as well.

Bias of the Public Authority Contemplating Paternalism

As already noted, Mill's aim in *On Liberty* is to devise a policy regarding the restriction of liberty that will be optimistic for actual conditions expected in modern societies, rather than for an imaginary ideal case. Mill's discussion does not abstract from the problems that beset a public authority contemplating paternalistic restriction due to the limited information at its disposal. Nor in trying to decide the merits of strict antipaternalism should we assume (a) that those subject to paternalist rules will comply perfectly with them, (b) that the administrative costs of paternalistic enforcement are insignificant or that the question of public funding of these costs poses no problems of efficiency or fairness, (c) that the officials charged with administering paternalistic rules will necessarily be motivated to carry out their duties in the spirit of the rules or that they will be competent to do so, or (d) that the public authority responsible for legislating paternalistic rules is itself motivated solely by impartial respect for principles of public morality.

Here I wish to raise the question whether or not the inappropriateness of making assumption (d) gives reason to think that strict antipaternalism is an expedient of fairness not perhaps in all abstractly possible circumstances but in anticipated conditions in the modern world. Very roughly the argument would go as follows. A government effectively controlled by an elite segment of the more able and the better off agents is unlikely to have much sympathetic understanding of the conditions of life and requirements for happiness of the less able and the worse off members of society.[15] If such a government enacts paternalistic legislation, wittingly or unwittingly it will legislate in a high-handed manner that is not likely to advance the supposed beneficiaries of the legislation. Strict antipaternalism is then a hedge against the benevolence of the crocodiles. In the event that a democratic government is effectively ruled by a majority of citizens, the suspicion of bias in the legislature now suggests legislative bias against the minority of more able citizens. Again, the conclusion of this line of thought is that strict antipaternalism in the circumstances for which Mill proposed it is recommended, not condemned, by fairness.

These conjectures do not succeed in establishing a case for the fairness of strict antipaternalism. First, if we assume a minority elite government biassed toward its own self-interest, this bias would appear to be just as likely to express itself in selfish laissez-faire as in selfish pseudopaternalism. No presumption in favor of antipaternalism emerges from this train of thought. Second, the introduction of majority rule political processes in itself has no discernible tendency that I can perceive to increase the likelihood that any paternalist legislation will reflect a bias against a distinct minority of more able citizens. It all depends on the relation between the distribution of prudential ability among the citizens and the voting blocs that are likely to coalesce into majority coalitions of voters. Prior to investigation the conjecture that a majority of more able votes will vote against a minority of the less able down and out looks just as plausible. Third, even if a sophisticated political sociology did inform us that in a given society majority rule is likely to produce paternalist legislation that favors the interests of the less able over the interests of the more able, a welfare egalitarian may view this tendency with cautious approval so long as it works in practise to further equality of welfare at acceptable cost of overall welfare.

It's His Fault

Consider the commonsense view that we do no injustice to a person if we decline to aid him by coercive interference with his liberty against his will, at least when the harm he will suffer in the absence of our intervention will be due to his own fault. The varieties of welfare egalitarianism that I have deployed against Mill all systematically ignore the fault of the agent as a determinant of his welfare in recommending the fairness of equal distribution of welfare (or the greater priority of advancing the welfare of the worse off). Paying no heed to such an extreme conception of fairness in his argument for the liberty principle, Mill stands on the firm ground of common sense, one might hold.

My criticism of Mill can accommodate the common sense view just mentioned. I need not contest the notion that a person can come to grief through his own doing, in such a manner that society owes him no compensation and bears no responsibility for the mess that the individual has made of his life simply by virtue of having granted him freedom which he has abused. Suppose we accept a principle of equality which states. "Other things equal it is a bad thing if social arrangements render some persons worse off than others through no fault of their own."[16] Whatever conception of fault one adopts, inequalities of welfare that arise through the individual's own fault as judged by that conception will neither violate the principle of equality nor count as unfair.

But on anybody's conception of fault the prudential disabilities that separate more and less able agents are surely in very considerable part due to accidents of genetic endowment and variously favorable early childhood circumstances that do not lie within the agent's control and for which he cannot be either praiseworthy or blameworthy. So even if we accept that it is sensible to attribute some prudential failings of individuals to personal fault, these attributions cannot reconcile us to regarding as fair the great bulk of inequalities of welfare that separate more and less able agents. Paternalism remains in the running as one morally appropriate response to some of these pervasive and disquieting inequalities. Nothing in *On Liberty* should assuage this sense of disquiet.

II. Feinberg's Soft Antipaternalism

Voluntary Choice

So far I have not considered the common position that is usually labelled "soft paternalism" and that Joel Feinberg prefers to call "soft antipaternalism". Since Feinberg's recent volume, *Harm to Self*, in his magisterial work on *The Moral Limits of the Criminal Law* is in my opinion the best work on paternalism that we have, my discussion of this position focuses on his analysis.[17]

Feinberg argues that what is wrong with paternalistic restriction of liberty is that it violates a compelling ideal of personal autonomy, but that paternalistic restriction of action proceeding from choice that is substantially nonvoluntary does not violate the agent's autonomy, hence may sometimes be permissible. We might say that interference with substantially nonvoluntary conduct does not constitute restriction of a person's liberty against his will. A "substantially nonvoluntary" choice of action is one that departs too far from the ideal of a perfectly voluntary choice. Feinberg renders this ideal as follows: the choice of an adult person is perfectly voluntary if and only if (1) the chooser is competent (not insane, severely mentally retarded, or comatose), (2) the choice is not made under coercion or duress, (3) the choice is not made "because of more subtle manipulation" (such as posthypnotic suggestion), (4) the chooser is not making his choice because of ignorance or mistaken belief about the circumstances in which he acts or the likely consequences of the various alternative actions open to him, and (5) the chooser "does not choose in circumstances that are temporarily distorting" ("not impetuously {on impulse]; not while fatigued; not while excessively nervous, agitated, or excited; not under the influence of a powerful passion, e.g. rage, hatred, lust, or a gripping mood, e.g. depression, mania; not under the influence of mind-numbing drugs, e.g. alcohol; not in pain, e.g. headache; not a neurotically compulsive or obsessive choice; not made under severe time pressures") [p. 115]. In short, a perfectly voluntary choice is one that is not marred by any of a miscellaneous set of features that tend to prevent choice from "faithfully representing" the agent "in an important way, expressing his settled values and preferences."[18]

To determine whether a particular choice falls too far short of this ideal to be voluntary enough to be appropriately protected by antipaternalist principle, Feinberg urges that we apply a variable standard depending on the situation. To appreciate the rationale of a variable standard, note that the point of soft antipaternalism is not to prevent the doing of actions of low degrees of voluntariness as such, but rather "to prevent people from suffering harm that they have not truly chosen to suffer or to risk suffering" (p. 119).

Finally, Feinberg reminds us that sometimes restriction of individual liberty in self-regarding matters is needed to establish whether or not action is proceeding from choice that is voluntary enough in the circumstances. The principle of soft antipaternalism thus holds: "The state has the right to prevent self-regarding harmful conduct when but only when it is substantially nonvoluntary, or when temporary intervention is necessary to establish whether it is nonvoluntary or not" (p. 126).

Solving the Problem?

To some extent this soft antipaternalist position assumes away the limiting conditions on choice of principle that persuade Mill to embrace (less than wholeheartedly, it is true) hard antipaternalism. Mill writes, "It is easy for any one to imagine an ideal public, which leaves the freedom and choice of individuals in all uncertain matters undisturbed, and only requires them to abstain from modes of conduct which universal experience has condemned. But where has there been seen a public which set any such limit to its censorship?" (pp. 283–284). As Mill formulates the problem, we are to determine the best constitutional norm for the guidance of such legislators as we are likely to get, not a norm that would be best for ideal legislators of our imagining. We are also evidently meant to assume severe limitations on the extent to which the legislature can tailor its restrictions to the different decision-making and decision-executing abilities of its citizens. If we could exactly tailor restrictive social laws to individual deficiencies, we could do the best for each citizen, and the tradeoffs between the welfare of the worse off and the welfare of the better off that I have envisaged would not be necessary, so neither would fairness problems arise in resolving such tradeoff issues. We have to ask whether soft antipaternalism's way of assuming away the problem should count as solution or evasion of the difficulty.

Feinberg suggests two procedures for tailoring legal rules to individual levels of competence. One is to exempt agents who act soft-paternalistically with good reason from the ordinary civil and criminal law penalties to which they might otherwise be liable (pp. 154, 157). For example, the law might specify that a good Samaritan who intervenes forcibly to prevent an acquaintance from ingesting a drug that will harm him is exempt from liability to a criminal charge of battery. Another suggested procedure, urged in connection with the idea of placing persons who initiate or threaten self-harming actions under temporary restraint for the purpose of establishing whether the choice of these acts would be substantially nonvoluntary, is to institute commissions of inquiry and the like for deciding such matters (pp. 125–126, 128).

The first suggestion strikes me as sensible, though its impact in increasing the sensitivity of paternalistic restriction to individual cases is likely to be limited. If the suggestion were implemented, the law would permit but not require soft-paternalistic intervention by persons who are well-placed to make a sound judgment about the case at hand. Surrounded by neighbours and strangers who would rather not get involved, the individual in need of rescue would be unlikely to get it. One's chances of rescue from substantially nonvoluntary self-damaging courses of action would depend largely on the astuteness, caring, and decisiveness of one's friends, relatives, and acquaintances. Notice also that due to assortative mating and more broadly the tendency for people to associate with others of similar accomplishment and status, the better off may stand to gain more than the worse off from criminal-law permission of private paternalistic interference.

In contrast, the proposal to establish voluntariness-determining boards of inquiry appears to be of dubious utility. Reliable evidence about such matters would be hard to come by—more difficult, I should think, than the problem that arises in criminal trials of determining whether the accused person's conduct is voluntary enough to establish his personal responsibility for it. Whether the reasons for doing what one proposes to do are confused or mistaken depends on the goal one hopes to achieve, so a person intent on establishing her right to do what she wants would have a strong incentive to dissemble about her intended goal and to present cooked-up, reasonable-sounding but sham reasons for her proposed course of action. Such dissembling would be difficult to detect. A negative verdict on the voluntary character of an individual's proposed course of action in a self-regarding matter would in the nature of the case often inflict a severely humiliating blow on the self-esteem of the individual. Such a finding by an official state agency would be bound to carry the sting of insult. Moreover, the fact-finding boards would be expensive to administer and would have difficulty convincing the general public of the reliability and consistency of their procedures. Enforcing the negative verdicts of these boards would be difficult and expensive, but necessary if the boards are not to arouse public contempt. Apparently what the soft antipaternalist envisages is selective prohibition of activities: whereas the use of dangerous recreational drugs, for instance, would not be generally prohibited, use of such drugs would be forbidden to people whose choice of drug usage was deemed nonvoluntary. One pictures a bureaucratic nightmare. Under current law we do selectively prohibit certain activities, as by FDA rules that forbid the purchase and consumption of certain drugs except with a doctor's prescription, but in this example the standards used to decide who is prohibited from engaging in the activity and who is not are reasonably uncontroversial and application of the standards by medical experts does not (usually!) give rise to intractable dispute. It is unlikely in the extreme that either of these conditions would be met if the system of leaving the determination of individual voluntariness to state boards of inquiry were instituted. This proposal looks to be of doubtful utility, and to be very unlikely substantially to reduce the screening problem that sets Mill's agenda.[19]

It should be noted that the extent of one's willingness to support the proposal to institute voluntariness-determining boards of inquiry despite its administrative cumbersomeness, likely high cost, and low prospect of delivering reliable verdicts will depend on the extent of one's commitment to the value of personal autonomy. The more one regards it as a terrible thing for the state or society to infringe the personal autonomy of an individual citizen acting voluntarily enough in a self-regarding matter, the more one will reasonably be willing to bear the moral costs of governmental procedures that attempt to discriminate voluntary and nonvoluntary self-harming actions for the purpose of leaving the one free while restricting the other. To settle accounts decisively with soft antipaternalism will require an evaluation of the ideal of personal autonomy that the soft antipaternalist is concerned above all to defend. (On this, see the final subsection of this paper).

There turns out to be no adequate reason for assuming that paternalistic rules can always be made variable in their application depending on individual determinations of decision-making competence. (To clarify: Feinberg himself does not make this assumption). The problem that I have raised for the hard antipaternalist must be faced by the soft antipaternalist as well.

Another Fairness Issue

The soft antipaternalist must face the issue of the fairness of the welfare-distributing impact of this proposed standard for justified paternalism. But given that the soft antipaternalist need not be committed to the maximization of utility come what may, I have so far given no reason to think that he must be committed in advance to a policy that is tilted toward increasing the welfare of the already better off segment of society at the expense of the already worse off. When incomplete information and the unfeasibility of perfect screening force us to treat a group of bad choosers and good choosers alike, either restricting all or restricting none, the soft antipaternalist would appear to be entirely free to use an appropriately distribution-weighted consequentialist principle (or for that matter a nonconsequentialist principle) in deciding whether or not to impose a restriction.[20]

This appearance strikes me as deceptive. The situation is confusing because soft antipaternalism is crucially vague. Once we try to pin down this vagueness, the position either reduces to single-party welfarist consequentialism (explained below) or it does not. If it does, I have no quarrel with the position except to note that the label is misleading advertising, because soft antipaternalism so construed dissolves into ordinary propaternalism. If it does not, then I contend that soft antipaternalism rests on a notion of personal sovereignty or personal autonomy that is bound to have undesirable distributive implications. Whereas my objection to Mill's antipaternalism is that it is too utilitarian, my objection to soft antipaternalism is that it is not utilitarian enough!

Welfarism and Soft Antipaternalism

By *Single-party welfarist consequentialism* I understand the view that insofar as we have to choose action for situations that involve no conflicts of interest among persons, but simply involve one person whose good might be advanced by what we do, in deciding how our action might best advance the person's good we are to be guided entirely by that very person's own conception of the good. Insofar as we are aiming to act for the good of another, that person's values, tastes, and preferences (perhaps corrected by hypothetical ideal deliberation) entirely determine the goal we should seek.[21]

The reason that soft antipaternalism tends to melt into plain oldfashioned paternalism is that its core idea of a substantially nonvoluntary choice is elusive, and not clearly distinct from the straight utility-maximizing notion of a choice that ought to be forcibly interfered with for the agent's own good. In sorting out these notions, some distinctions will prove helpful. First, we have the idea of a *nonoptimizing choice* by an agent, a choice that (if acted upon) would fail to maximize the agent's own rationally expected good, provided that this shortfall would not be counterbalanced by likely good effects of the agent's act on other persons. Of course the class of nonoptimizing choices does not coincide with the class of choices that on single-party welfare consequentialist grounds ought to be interfered with. After all, there may be no reliable way to improve on an agent's imperfect choice. Second, let us define a *substantially nonoptimizing choice* as one that (if acted upon) would fail to maximize the agent's good (without producing counterbalancing benefits for others) to such an extent and in circumstances such that paternalistically restricting the agent from acting on that choice would be feasible and, from the standpoint of maximizing the agent's own good, desirable.

A substantially nonvoluntary choice, according to Feinberg, is one that is not "voluntary enough", where being voluntary enough is a function of the degree that the choice falls short of perfect voluntariness, the likelihood that acting on the choice will bring harm, the magnitude of the harm thus risked, and the extent to which any harm that might be done will be irreversible. The function is not specified; this is evidently a matter to be left to the discretion of the reasonable legislator or other agent contemplating paternalistic intervention (p. 117). An imperfectly voluntary choice is one that fails to meet the standard of perfect voluntariness, but imperfectly voluntary choices may be optimizing and even if nonoptimizing, may not be substantially nonoptimizing.

The question I find it difficult to decide is whether the class of choices that are substantially nonvoluntary, hence not protected from paternalistic interference by the soft antipaternalist principle, coincides with the class of substantially nonoptimizing choices. Certainly the features of choices that by definition tend to render them substantially nonvoluntary are features that in fact tend to render them substantially nonoptimizing. The situation seems interpretively indeterminate.

Feinberg leaves us in no doubt that in his opinion soft antipaternalism does conflict in a morally significant way with the ordinary propaternalist position that paternalism is justified just in case it maximally promotes the good of the intended beneficiary (without involving counterbalancing excess costs to others). The crux of the matter in his view is whether one takes personal sovereignty as a constraint never to be violated (see, e.g., pp. 57–62, 157, 184–186). Whence this confidence of judgment? The explanation may be simply that I have been assuming so far that we understand the reference to the good of the agent in the definitions of "nonoptimizing choice" and "substantially nonoptimizing choice" in a welfarist way, as determined entirely by the agent's own personal values and preferences (perhaps as these would be corrected by ideal deliberation). With that assumption in place, it might seem that any paternalistic acts we propose will be justified by some failure of the agent either to take effective means to achieve her goals or to identify her goals in a reasonable way, without factual error, reasoning error, or emotional instability (but see the discussion in the next subsection). But these are all voluntariness-reducing features of choice.

However, if we drop that assumption, then the propaternalist may be a perfectionist who believes he knows what goods are objectively worth achieving and that restriction of a person's liberty to enable him to achieve more of those goods may be justifiable quite apart from any showing that the person's choices are imperfectly voluntary. From a perfectionist standpoint, there may be good ground for paternalistic restriction even of an agent's perfectly voluntary choice. From a welfarist standpoint, such grounds will be difficult to identify; there may be none.

Insofar as Feinberg's soft antipaternalism takes perfectionism as its target of opposition I have no quarrel with it. Nor do I dispute Feinberg's assertion that soft antipaternalism is significantly antipaternalist. But all of this leaves completely open the question that interests me: Whether the paternalism that could be justified on single-party welfarist consequentialist grounds differs at all from that paternalism that could be justified on soft antipaternalist grounds. This is the question to which, I claim, soft antipaternalism as worked out by Feinberg permits no determinate answer.

A brief digression will clarify what divides the welfarist and her perfectionist opponent. If the welfarist simply identifies a person's good with satisfaction of her actual preferences, the contrast with the perfectionist is obvious; so let us consider an ideal welfarist who takes it that a person may misidentify her "true" values. According to the ideal welfarist, a person's good is maximal satisfaction of the personal values and preferences that she would have if she were to reflect about this matter with full pertinent information, while making no reasoning errors, and in a calm mood. But the ideal welfarist is completely open-minded about the outcome of this ideal deliberation procedure and does not assume it likely that all persons would converge on the same values and preferences as ideal deliberation was approached. (This is one way to represent Mill's espousal of diversity and individuality in chapter 3 of *On Liberty*. We have different individual natures and to some extent the good for each of us may well vary). In contrast, the perfectionist can be represented as committed to the belief that as the limit of ideal deliberation about one's good was approached, all persons would converge in agreeing on a certain conception of human flourishing, which constitutes the objective good for humanity. The perfectionist is willing to impose paternalistically on a person who with full voluntariness affirms a conception of her good that disagrees with the perfectionist's notion of objective good. Charitably construed, such imposition rests on the conjecture that there would be convergence after ideal deliberation and that the view converged upon would be substantially the same as what the perfectionist now upholds. So interpreted, the perfectionist seems to me to be exuding unwarranted self-confidence about epistemic matters to which at present we have only very restricted and doubtful access.

Welfare versus Autonomy

I want tentatively to explore further the issue of whether there would be any important practical disagreement between soft antipaternalism and single-party welfarist consequentialism. I describe below three cases in which it might be plausible to suppose such disagreement might arise.

Self-abasing Benevolence. Imagine that a person chooses with perfect voluntariness to sacrifice a great amount of her own welfare for a small net increase in the welfare of others.[22] It is probably better to concentrate on examples of inefficient self-sacrificing behavior done for the purpose of benefitting strangers or acquaintances rather than close relatives or friends, because in some cases of the latter (e.g., a parent's sacrifice for a child) it can be very difficult to discern to what extent the agent's own self-interest encompasses the advantage of the person sacrificed for, so that in acting to benefit another one is also acting to benefit oneself. In cases of self-abasing benevolence the person seems to reveal a conviction that the welfare of others is more worthwhile than her own welfare, and this conviction need not be based on any factual error, error in reasoning, or the like. Nonetheless the fundamental welfarist idea is that, in Bentham's words, "Everybody is to count for one, nobody for more than one". No doubt a person's steady and abiding desire to benefit others even in ways that greatly diminish aggregate welfare typically could not be blocked from expressing itself except through draconian restriction of liberty that would itself do more harm than good. In some cases, however, the welfarist contemplating paternalistic intervention to stop self-abasing benevolence may correctly judge that forcible intervention, which strongly conveys to the restricted person the message, "We judge your welfare to be equally as worthwhile as anyone else's welfare", would itself shock the person in a way that imparts a greater belief in her own worth and destroys the propensity to benefit others at disproportionate cost to herself. In such cases the welfarist will recommend paternalistic restriction that the soft antipaternalist, I suggest, would on principle be required to eschew. Here I side with the welfarist against the soft antipaternalist.[23]

Voluntariness-reducing Factors in the Choice Situation That Are Themselves Voluntarily Chosen in Advance by the Agent. Suppose that in a cool hour one decides that if the boss refuses one's request for an increase in pay, one will say in reply spontaneously whatever comes into one's head, regardless of one's emotional state at that moment. Or suppose that a climber deliberately sets out on an adventurous climb under what look to be treacherous conditions, without consulting an available weather report that would certainly have a bearing on the safety of the planned enterprise. Her rationale for this apparant heedlessness is that she wishes to climb under conditions of extreme uncertainty, where some of the risks encountered are not known about in advance, so that she will have to exercise her wits and skill in a situation that will require quick and sure improvisation. A third sort of example occurs when gaining more information known to be relevant to a decision one is taking is itself painful for the agent. Suppose that you know that there is very little chance that learning about the safety hazards of your job will induce you to switch careers, but it is virtually certain that learning about such information and rendering it emotionally vivid to yourself will be distressing, perhaps to the point of inhibiting job performance. So one stops gathering job-safety information. It may be that if we fully describe these situations it will turn out that the supposition that the agent makes the advance decision with perfect voluntariness is contradictory. I am not sure about this, but I doubt it. Be that as it may, I note that we can imagine variants of the above stories in which a friend of the agent acquires information about the situation which renders it very probable that what the agent is planning to do will be substantially nonoptimizing. By welfarist standards, the friend would then be justified in intervening forcibly to restrict the agent's liberty for her own good. Here too there might be a conflict between the implications of soft antipaternalism and single-party welfarist consequentialism regarding the justifiability of paternalism in such cases.

Prior Restriction of the Choice Set That Partially Forms Individual Preferences.[24] Let us distinguish two kinds of paternalistic restriction of liberty: preventing someone from doing what he already wants to do, and preventing someone from ever entertaining the

option of doing a thing and forming a desire for it by prior restriction of the choice set. For this distinction to have any practical sig-
nificance, it must be assumed that people's basic preferences (what
one prefers for its own sake, not as a means to further aims) are partially determined by the range of initial options available to them.
A perhaps farfetched example illustrating the distinction would be
this: Suppose the government by dint of great restriction of liberty
of the present generation of smokers is able to enforce a completely
effective ban on smoking, so the practise completely disappears
after one generation. Ignore the possible unfairness to the first
generation and consider the effect of this entirely successful ban on
smoking on members of future generations. Let us suppose the
idea of smoking effectively dies out. People read about the practise, as an historical curiosity, but nobody sees others smoking, so
nobody ever forms the desire to smoke. I take it that with respect
to the later generations of nonsmokers, the ideal of personal sovereignty underlying soft antipaternalism would deem unacceptable
the coercive manipulation of people's choice sets in this fashion.
Such coercion will count as a factor that reduces the voluntariness
of people's nonchoice of smoking. Personal sovereignty is
assaulted just as much by coercion that reduces that voluntariness
of people's choices in self-regarding matters as by coercion that
prevents people from acting on their voluntary self-regarding
actions. If this is so, then we have here another possible instance of
practical disagreement between the single-party welfarist consequentialist and the soft antipaternalist.

   None of the cases described above seems very clear-cut to me.
Hence I remain unsure whether soft antipaternalism really does end
up being extensionally equivalent to single-party welfarist consequentialism or not. I want nonetheless to explore the possibility that
the two views really do conflict and that soft antipaternalism condemns acts of paternalism that are justifiable on welfarist grounds.

Two Conceptions of Autonomy

The problem for the soft antipaternalist as I see it is this. We are
to imagine that an individual's choice is substantially nonopti-

mizing, which means that paternalistic interference can improve on the expected outcome that is foreseeable if the individual is permitted to act on that choice. Moreover, paternalism can improve on the expected outcome as that would be judged from the self-interested standpoint of the individual whose conduct we propose to restrict. We propose to restrict the individual's self-regarding freedom in order to advance goals that the individual herself either is seeking to fulfill or would seek after ideal deliberation. In the name of personal sovereignty the soft antipaternalist opposes interference. Despite the fact that paternalism would advance the agent's own conception of her good, the agent's choice is voluntary enough, so the right of personal sovereignty trumps the agent's good. The individual's sovereignty over her own life gives her the absolute right that her liberty to carry out a voluntary choice in a self-regarding matter should never be coercively restricted for paternalistic reasons—so says the soft antipaternalist.

But the agent's own conception of her good will presumably include a conception of autonomy or personal sovereignty and a weighting of this good against other goods that the agent values for herself. If the agent's choice really is substantially nonoptimizing, then paternalism can better advance the agent's good than her own execution of her own choice, where this good of the agent includes her own relative ranking of autonomy against other values. On what ground does the soft antipaternalist override the agent's own placing of autonomy in her personal scheme of values? From a single-party welfarist consequentialist standpoint, this insistence that "autonomy trumps" is just another species of perfectionist imposition of values on the agent in defiance of the agent's own considered evaluation. To take an extreme case, an agent might conceivably have personal values and preferences that assign strict lexical priority to the desire never to be subjected to paternalistic interference not justified by soft antipaternalist standards. In this case, the welfarist and the soft antipaternalist will agree that if the agent's choice is "voluntary enough", so that this overriding desire for autonomy comes into play, no paternalism against the dictates of soft antipaternalism could be justified.[25] But if the agent does not happen to have this extreme weighting of preferences, why does respect for her autonomy plausibly require giving greater weight to her autonomy than she herself gives it? An alternate way to put this point is to note that welfarist consequentialism has its own notion of autonomy—namely, insofar as one is trying to further an agent's good, be guided by that very agent's conception of good and nothing else.[26] It is far from clear that, having conceded so much to this conception, the soft antipaternalist can successfully defend a rival view of autonomy or sovereignty.

Feinberg skillfully characterizes the soft antipaternalist ideal of personal sovereignty in terms of a comparison to the sovereignty of states (pp. 47–57). A political metaphor is at work here. Just as a state is sovereign over its territory and has the right that its sovereignty not be infringed, so the individual is sovereign over his own life, or more exactly over his self-regarding actions, and has the right of self-rule that should be just as inviolate as state sovereignty. The political metaphor is supposed to clarify the concept of personal sovereignty even if we have doubts that states morally are entitled to the strong rights of sovereignty they have claimed. The ideal of personal sovereignty is that individuals should have the sovereignty over their own lives that states have claimed (rightly or wrongly) over their own territory (p. 51).

But soft antipaternalism as characterized by Feinberg actually backs away from this bold claim. The sovereignty that states claim is surely not the right that their substantially voluntary choices should not be subject to forcible external interference. Suppose the legitimate government of some country enacts some policy that will affect only its own citizens, and is enthusiastically supported by them, but is in fact a stupid policy that will defeat the goals that the government clearly announces and that the citizens foolishly believe will be served by it. Our ordinary notion of political sovereignty holds that a benevolent neighboring nation is not entitled in these circumstances to send its troops over the border in a surgical raid that will correct this self-defeating policy and inaugurate an imposed policy better calculated to achieve the goals the government and citizens so clearly desire. Political sovereignty entitles a nation to make its own mistakes and wallow in the consequences of its own stupidity at least where only its own citizens are directly harmed thereby. Personal sovereignty as explicated by Feinberg is different in this respect. According to Feinberg's idea of personal sovereignty, an individual's self-regarding choice that threatens harm to himself and falls "too far" short of perfect voluntariness may be subject to coercive interference on paternalistic grounds, consistently with personal sovereignty. But why not then let the individual's own values fully determine when paternalistic interference may justifiably be executed, consistently with personal sovereignty?[27] Soft antipaternalism seems to be an unacceptable half-way house.

Moreover, to return at last to the issue of distributive fairness, it is easy to see that imputing to individuals a strict lexical preference never to suffer paternalistic interference in violation of the soft antipaternalist principle, regardless of individuals' own evaluations of this matter, will predictably work to the advantage of the haves and to the disadvantage of the have-nots. Good choosers will predictably fare better under a regime of soft antipaternalism than bad choosers, because the imposed value of sovereignty will be more likely to constrain the state or other would-be interferers from carrying out paternalistic acts that really will work to the benefit of the latter. The distributive dimension of the paternalism issue, hitherto largely ignored, is significant. Once acknowledged, it cuts against the advocacy of any form of strict antipaternalism.[28]

Notes

1. This definition needs further refinement, but will serve my purposes. As usually understood, antipaternalism forbids restricting a person's liberty for her own good against her present will, unless her present will is bound by voluntary prior commitment. On the definition of paternalism, see Gerald DWORKIN, "Paternalism" and "Paternalism: Some Second Thoughts", both in *Paternalism*, ed. Rolf Sartorius (Minneapolis, University of Minnesota Press, 1983), pp. 19–22 and 105–107; also my "Mill versus Paternalism", *Ethics* 90 (July, 1980): 470–489: see esp. pp. 471–472. For a good criticism of my suggestion, along with many other instructive observations, see Joel FEINBERG, *The Moral Limits of the Criminal Law*, vol. 3, *Harm to Self* (Oxford and New York, Oxford University Press, 1986), pp. 3–23.

2. On the question of whether Mill intended the liberty principle to forbid enforced charity, see D. G. BROWN, "Mill on Liberty and Morality", *Philosophical Review* 81 (1972): 133–158; David LYONS, "Liberty and Harm to Others", *Canadian Journal of Philosophy*, supp. vol. 5 (1979), pp. 1–19; and Fred BERGER, *Happiness, Justice*

and Freedom: The Moral and Political Philosophy of John Stuart Mill (Berkeley and Los Angeles, The University of California Press, 1984), pp. 253–258.

3. See Henry David AIKEN, "Utilitarian and Liberty: John Stuart Mill's Defense of Freedom", in his *Reason and Conduct: New Bearings in Moral Philosophy* (New York, Alfred A. Knopf, 1962), pp. 292–314. See also the references cited in footnote 17 of chapter 1 of John GRAY's *Mill on Liberty: A Defence* (London, Routledge and Kegan Paul, 1983), pp. 131–132. C. L. TEN tries to show "that Mill's case for liberty is not wholly reconcilable with any consistent version of utilitarianism" and defends the nonutilitarian libertarianism he imputes to Mill in *Mill on Liberty* (Oxford, Oxford University Press, 1980). See especially the summary of his argument on p. 9, from which the quotation above is taken. See also FEINBERG, *Harm to Self*, pp. 57–62.

4. FEINBERG, *Harm to Self*. (Further page references to this work are in parentheses in the text).

5. John Stuart MILL, *On Liberty*, in *Collected Works*, vol. 5, ed. J. M. Robson (Toronto and Buffalo, University of Toronto Press, 1977), p. 283. (Further page references to this work are in parentheses in the text.)

6. Two clarifications are needed here. First, my argument does not require the assumption that any paternalistic rule that is justified as promoting the utility of its intended beneficiaries (agents who would otherwise harm themselves) must benefit the less able to a greater extent than it benefits the more able. There might be a self-regarding vice to which more able agents are peculiarly susceptible and the bad effects of this vice might be correctible by paternalism. All that my argument requires is that on the whole and on the average, paternalistic rules will be more to the advantage of less able agents. Second, my argument does not require the assumption either that the less able agents are always among the worse off or that paternalism (when justified as above) is never more to the advantage of better off agents. Both these assumptions are evidently false. A person who is very inept at managing his life may nevertheless be blessed by external advantages, such as wealth and wise friends, which insulate him from the bad effects toward which his self-regarding faults tend. And there might be self-regarding vices (such as consumption of very expensive but dangerously harmful recreational drugs) to which people who have better than average welfare prospects are peculiarly liable. In this regard my argument requires only the assumption that on the whole and on the average, being among the less able identifies an individual as facing below-average welfare prospects.

7. A maximin welfare policy holds that institution should be arranged so as to maximize the welfare of the worst off. On maximin and on its leximin extension see Amartya SEN, "Equality of What ?", reprinted in his *Choice, Welfare and Measurement* (Oxford, Basil Blackwell, 1982), pp. 353–369. On weighted utilitarianism, see Paul WEIRICH, "Utility Tempered with Equality", *Nous* 17 (1983), 423–439. On effective average, see Nicholas RESCHER, *Distributive Justice: A Constructive Critique of the Utilitarian Theory of Distribution* (Indianapolis, Bobbs-Merrill Co., 1966), pp. 31–38.

8. The statement in the text is not quite right. The three views mentioned in the previous footnote all give greater weight to increasing the welfare of the worse off than to increasing the welfare of the better off. But if the position of those below average in welfare cannot be improved, a principle of equality of welfare would be averse to increasing the welfare of the better off, but weighted utilitarianism and leximin version of maximin would favor such improvement even though it increases inequality.

9. Gerald DWORKIN, "Paternalism", p. 22.

10. Bernard WILLIAMS, "A Critique of Utilitarianism", in *Utilitarianism For and Against*, J. J. C. Smart and Bernard Williams (Cambridge, Cambridge University Press, 1973), p. 113.

11. On this point, see BERGER, pp. 267–268, and FEINBERG, pp. 71–79.

12. Robert GOODIN, "Anticipating Evaluations: Saving People From Their Former Selves", chapter 3 in his *Political Theory and Public Policy* (Chicago, University of Chicago Press, 1982), pp. 39–47, discusses common defects in people's incorporation of risky and uncertain prospects into their decisionmaking.

13. See the discussions of Mill's bridge-crossing example in GRAY, pp. 91–92, FEINBERG, pp. 124–127, and C. L. TEN, pp. 109–117. These authors believe the drift of this passage is toward soft antipaternalism, but for convenience I ignore this possible reading of Mill and postpone discussion of soft antipaternalism to section II.

14. See *Rational Choice: The Contrast between Economics and Psychology*, eds. Robin M. Hogarth and Melvin W. Reder (Chicago and London, The University of Chicago Press, 1986). See also Richard THALER, "The Psychology of Choice and the Assumptions of Economics", Working Paper RR-3, Center for Philosophy and Public Policy, University of Maryland.

15. See John Stuart MILL, *Considerations on Representative Government*, in *Collected Works*, vol. 19., ed. J. M. Robson (Toronto and Buffalo, University of Toronto Press, 1977), p. 405.

16. This formulation is borrowed from Derek PARFIT, *Reasons and Persons* (Oxford, Oxford University Press, 1984), p. 26.

17. Besides *Harm to Self*, FEINBERG'S *The Moral Limits of the Criminal Law* includes two other published volumes, *Harm to Others* (1984), and *Offense to Others* (1985). A fourth volume, *Harmless Wrongdoing*, is forthcoming.

My discussion of soft antipaternalism is heavily indebted to Dan BROCK, "Paternalism and Promoting the Good", in *Paternalism*, ed. Rolf Sartorius, pp. 237–260. See also Daniel WIKLER, "Paternalism and the Mildly Retarded", *Philosophy and Public Affairs* 8 (1979): 377–392. I am also indebted to Feinberg's good criticisms of some of my own earlier thoughts on this topic, pp. 128–132.

18. But as Feinberg observes, a person may with perfect voluntariness make a choice that is out of character or that goes against her hitherto settled values and preferences. For a discussion of paternalism that defends strong paternalism when it protects the agent from choices that fail adequately to represent faithfully her settled values, see John KLEINIG, *Paternalism* (Totowa, N.J., Rowman and Allanheld, 1983), chapter 3.

19. The doubts that I raise about the likely usefulness of state boards of inquiry for determining voluntariness do not extend to the ordinary practise of allowing state agents to intervene forcibly to determine whether apparently nonvoluntary action really is so—for example, checking to see if the person is acting on obvious and choice-determining factual ignorance, as in Mill's bridge-crossing example, or to see if the person is acting under the influence of alcohol or another choice-distorting drug.

20. Feinberg discusses examples that turn on the unfeasibility of perfect screening of good choosers from bad choosers at pp. 18–21 and p. 128. He does not suggest that the liberty of the good choosers must take priority when protecting their liberty must be at the expense of the welfare of bad choosers, who could be helped by an inclusive paternalistic rule.

21. On hypothetical ideal deliberation as determining the preferences that constitute a person's good, see Richard B. BRANDT, *A Theory of the Good and the Right* (Oxford, Oxford University Press, 1979), pp. 110–129; and David GAUTHIER, *Morals by Agreement* (Oxford, Oxford University Press, 1986), pp. 26–32.

22. See Michael SLOTE, "Morality and Self-Other Asymmetry", *Journal of Philosophy* 81 (1984): 179–192.

23. Notice, however, that a broader range of cases must be considered than is included in this discussion. Suppose that a person with perfect voluntariness chooses to dedicate herself to a goal, such as saving the whales from extinction, that is not sought as part of her own happiness or as part of the happiness of other people. I do not wish a welfarist principle to justify paternalism in such a case, but I cannot consider here the complications that must be introduced to attain this result. See my "Equality and Equal Opportunity for Welfare", forthcoming in *Philosophical Studies*.

24. This topic is considered from another viewpoint in Jon Elster, "Sour Grapes", chapter 3 in *Sour Grapes: Studies in the Subversion of Rationality* (Cambridge, Cambridge University Press, 1983), pp. 109–140.

25. On this point I have learned from Danny Scoccia's Ph.D. dissertation, on file at the University of California at San Diego Library.

26. Cf. John Harsanyi's notion of "preference autonomy"—"the principle that, in deciding what is good and what is bad for a given individual, the ultimate criterion can only be his own wants and his own preferences". See John HARSANYI, "Morality and the Theory of Rational Behavior", in *Utilitarianism and Beyond*, eds. Amartya Sen and Bernard Williams (Cambridge, Cambridge University Press, 1982), pp. 39–62; see esp. p. 55.

27. This question is not rhetorical. We need to distinguish two cases. When the soft antipaternalist eschews paternalist intervention that would effectively promote the fulfillment of the person's actual preferences, the preference autonomy case for intervention is clear and, to my mind, persuasive. But suppose the person's actual preferences are not well considered, and the ideal welfarist proposes paternalist intervention in order effectively to promote the fulfillment of the preferences the person would have after ideal deliberation. These nonactual preferences may seem a more doubtful basis for intervention. I suggest that in this case the preferences that determine a person's good are the preferences she would have if she were to deliberate about her preferences in an ideal way with full information *including pertinent information about her actual resistance to advice regarding the rationality of her preferences, the likelihood that her actual preferences will ever approximate to her ideally considered preferences, the costs of bringing about preference change toward her ideally considered preferences, and so on.* Only in (the rare) cases where the person contemplating paternalistic intervention has a strong epistemic warrant for claiming to know the person's hypothetical ideally considered preferences will appeal to these preferences justify such intervention.

28. This point has implications which cannot be developed here. I believe that any credible distributive egalitarianism will require assumptions that will tend to undermine any strict advocacy of antipaternalism. See in this regard Kai Nielsen's vigorous criticism of Robert Nozick's libertarianism, in *Equality and Liberty: A Defense of Radical Egalitarianism* (Totowa, N.J., Rowman and Allanheld, 1985), part IV. Nielsen's discussion does not challenge Nozick's antipaternalism.

6

Liberty and Harm to Others

David Lyons

This paper is part of an extended program of research[1] with two aims: to understand Mill's moral and political philosophy, and to develop a utilitarian doctrine in its most plausible or least vulnerable form, in order to identify what, if anything, may reasonably be said for or against utilitarianism as a general type of doctrine. These aims fit together because I have found when trying to interpret Mill that he suggests lines of development somewhat different and in some ways more promising than the usual versions of utilitarianism.

The Principle of Liberty is not a simple corollary of utilitarianism, and Mill argues for it. I am not concerned with his arguments for it, however, so much as I am with his applications of it, since they tell us how it is to be understood. The Principle of Liberty is like a Principle of Utility in that nonmoral conditions involving human welfare are given as justifying conduct. But the Principle of Liberty is narrower than a Principle of Utility, in at least two ways: it concerns harms to others, not welfare generally, and it concerns coercive intervention, not action generally.

Discussions of the Principle of Liberty often seem to get off on the wrong foot and to lack the scholarly charity that we usually confer on philosophical writing that is considered worth reading. I hope to rectify that sort of error here. I hope to show that the Principle of Liberty is more acceptable than it might otherwise seem, though I do not pretend to offer an unqualified defense of it.

I. Mill's Principle

Mill's Principle of Liberty asserts

> that the sole end for which mankind are warranted, individually
> or collectively, in interfering with the liberty of action of any of
> their number is self-protection. That the only purpose for which
> power can be rightfully exercised over any member of a civilized
> community, against his will, is to prevent harm to others. [1, 9][2]

The prevention of harm to others is regarded by Mill as a good
reason, and the only good reason, for "compulsion and control" of
the individual, or, in other words, for the direction of behavior by
threats, penalties, and force. [1,9]

In the course of his initial presentation of this principle, Mill
offers some examples of interference it would allow. He begins
with the obvious case: "If anyone does an act hurtful to others,
there is a *prima facie* case for punishing him by law or, where legal
penalties are not safely applicable, by general disapprobation."
[1,11] Not all such conduct should be prohibited, since there can
be overriding reasons against doing so. Sometimes, for example,
"the attempt to exercise control would produce other evils,
greater than those which it would prevent." [1,11] This suggests
that coercive regulations are required by Mill not just to prevent
harm, but to do so efficiently or economically. In any case, conduct that is harmful to others is clearly subject to control under
Mill's principle. And one must suppose that the same is true of
conduct that threatens to cause harm—reckless driving, say, as
well as bodily assault.

But Mill does not stop there. The passage continues with other
examples of justified "compulsion and control." Mill says:

> There are also many positive acts for the benefit of others which he
> may rightfully be compelled to perform, such as to give evidence
> in a court of justice, to bear his fair share in the common defense or
> in any other joint work necessary to the interest of the society of
> which he enjoys the protection, and to perform certain acts of indi-
> vidual beneficence, such as saving a fellow creature's life or inter-
> posing to protect the defenseless against ill-usage—things which

whenever it is obviously a man's duty to do he may rightfully be made responsible to society for not doing. [1,11]

I shall refer to these examples by saying that, in Mill's view, one may legitimately be required (at least in certain circumstances) to cooperate in joint undertakings and to act as a good samaritan.

These examples are presented by Mill as coercive requirements that would be permitted by his principle. D. G. Brown has argued, however, that they clash with it instead; and, partly for this reason, he has suggested that the Principle of Liberty is untenable.[3] Brown believes

> that we have duties to help other people which go beyond the avoidance of harming them; that the performance of such duties can legitimately be extracted from us, very commonly in our roles as citizens and taxpayers; and that such exactions are not permitted by Mill's main principle. (p. 158)[4]

Brown reasons in this way because he believes that Mill's Principle of Liberty does not allow interference unless the conduct that is interfered with can itself be considered harmful[5] to other persons. Such a principle would allow restrictions against bodily assault and reckless driving, for example, but it would not sanction either cooperation or good samaritan requirements.

Brown's interpretation of Mill is important because it forms part of a systematic study of Mill's doctrines, developed with reasonable charity. Brown furthermore avoids two errors that are commonly found in commentaries on Mill. He does not assume without question the textbook reading of Mill as an "act utilitarian," as one who holds that our sole or overriding moral obligation is to maximize utility. And he does not allow his interpretation of Mill's Principle of Liberty to get bogged down in discussions of Mill's distinction between "self-regarding" conduct (a term used by Mill) and "other-regarding" conduct (a term not even used by him). Brown proceeds, more usefully, to consider Mill's actual statement of the Principle as well as his substantive applications of it. I believe, however, that Brown is mistaken about Mill's views on several important points, and I shall here defend a different reading of the Principle of Liberty.

On the reading I propose, freedom may be limited only for the purpose of preventing harm to other persons, but the conduct that is interfered with need not itself be considered harmful or dangerous to others. Such a principle both conforms to Mill's definitive statement and accommodates his examples. The cooperation and good samaritan requirements that Mill refers to could not be justified on the ground that they prevent conduct that causes harm to others; but it can be argued that such regulations nevertheless work in other ways to prevent harm to others. This version of Mill's principle is one that he could readily endorse. It does justice to his own intentions and stays within the limits of his general position on morality and politics. Most importantly, it seems a more plausible principle than the one that Brown attributes to Mill, and one to be preferred by someone who accepts the idea that harm-prevention justifies "compulsion and control." But I shall stop short of claiming unequivocally that this principle is what Mill must have had in mind. The text suggests that Mill is, in fact, confused about some of the relevant differences between these versions of his Principle of Liberty and fails to face these issues squarely.

My argument proceeds as follows. In Section II I discuss the differences between Brown's version of the principle and mine and show how Mill's examples can be accommodated. In Section III I consider the problem of deciding which version best fits Mill's text. In Section IV I go beyond Brown's argument and deal with other difficulties for the reading I propose, including other reasons for thinking that Mill's own examples cannot be accommodated.

II. Harm Prevention

Mill's principle, we have seen, allows interference with conduct that is itself harmful or dangerous to others, such as bodily assault and reckless driving. So much is certain. But harm to others can be prevented not just by interfering with acts that can be said to cause, or that threaten to cause, harm to other persons, and the other possibilities are extremely important.

Consider good samaritan requirements. When someone has been injured or is in danger, harm (or further harm) to him might be averted if another person comes to his aid. It makes no difference here what, if anything, can be said to cause the harm or danger. If the Principle of Liberty says flatly (as on my reading it does) that the prevention of harm to others justifies interfering with my liberty, then it might justify interfering with my liberty in this sort of case. I might be required to come to another's aid, in order to prevent harm to him, even if I may not be said to have caused the harm that he will suffer if I should fail to help him when I can. In such cases, it cannot be assumed that someone who fails to help prevent harm can be said to cause the harm. Suppose, for example, that I am in a position to save a drowning man. If I fail to do so, I will have failed to prevent harm to him. But it does not follow that my failure can be said to cause the harm. For, as Brown observes (p. 145), the drowning man may have tried to take his own life or may have been pushed by a third party, in which cases the harm done would not be attributable to me, even though I failed to intervene. In sum, lives can be saved and injuries minimized—harm to others can be prevented—not only by interfering with, preventing, or otherwise suppressing harmful and dangerous conduct but also by requiring or otherwise eliciting helpful, harm-preventing conduct. This would seem to be the very point of one class of Mill's examples, in which we would be required "to perform certain acts of individual beneficence, such as saving a fellow creature's life or interposing to protect the defenseless against ill-usage."

Brown formulates Mill's Principle of Liberty as follows:

(L) The liberty of action of the individual ought *prima facie* to be interfered with if and only if his conduct is harmful to others. (p. 135)

In other words, there is only one good reason for interfering with a person's conduct, namely, that the conduct is harmful (or dangerous) to others. This may be called a *harmful conduct-prevention principle*. It does not allow interference except with conduct that causes (or at least threatens) harm to others. It would not sanction good samaritan requirements.

Mill's definitive statement of his principle is not so restricted. It can be understood to say:

(L*) The prevention of harm to other persons is a good reason, and the only good reason, for restricting behavior.

This may be called a *general harm-prevention principle*. It would not exclude good samaritan requirements. Someone who believes that there may be circumstances in which one may justifiably be required to come to others' aid, even though one is not responsible for their difficulties, should prefer a general harm-prevention principle, like (L*), to a narrower harmful conduct-prevention principle, like (L).

Another important class of cases is represented by cooperation requirements. Like good samaritan requirements, these would not normally be thought of as interfering with conduct that causes harm to others. But these are unlike good samaritan requirements, and thus warrant separate treatment, because they typically require acts that would not normally be credited, at least in the same direct way, with preventing harm. The prevention of harm to others here is more a function of the requirements themselves or of the patterns of behavior they create. Furthermore, in many such cases, each member of the community stands to benefit from the regulations—oneself as well as others, though only the benefits to others are relevant in justifying restrictions on one's conduct under the Principle of Liberty.

Consider Mill's example of being required to give testimony in court. How is harm prevented here? It is true that giving testimony in compliance with a subpoena can sometimes be credited with preventing harm to others, as when it secures for someone an acquittal against a criminal charge or a successful defense against a damage claim. But it is unlikely that Mill meant or we would want to limit a subpoena rule to just such cases. One would presumably wish it to apply (as it does now), for example, to prosecution witnesses in a criminal proceeding. Compliance with a general subpoena rule can just as readily have the opposite effect upon the individuals who are most directly involved—by securing a conviction, say, or ensuring a successful damage claim. The harm-prevention grounds for such a rule would not be like the case for good samaritan requirements.

If the requirement that one give testimony in court can be justified in harm-prevention terms, it is likely to be by reasoning of the following sort. Courts, though costly and burdensome, are needed to settle and prevent disputes and for an effective system of social regulations. Courts are needed to prevent evils that are worse than the evils they entail. (For simplicity, we should assume that the substantive rules to be enforced can themselves be justified in harm-prevention terms. Otherwise, a harm-prevention defense of court rules and operations would have to be qualified severely.) Various rules are required if courts are to operate effectively. One of these requires persons under certain circumstances to give testimony. It is needed as part of an institution that helps to prevent harm. It might thus be justified on the basis of harm-prevention, even though it cannot plausibly be treated as the prohibition of harmful or dangerous conduct. For the point of such a rule is not to interfere with conduct that would independently be characterized as harmful or dangerous to others, but is rather to redirect behavior so as to help create a social practice that will help prevent harm.

In this sort of case, the harm to be prevented may well be "public," that is, presumably affecting all the members of a community, neighborhood, or class, at least in the form of danger or insecurity. This means that one may very well stand to benefit from the regulation of one's own behavior. Benefits to oneself are, of course, irrelevant to the justification of a rule under the Principle of Liberty. But, from the fact that the harm is public it follows not only that one stands to benefit but also that others benefit too, and this fact makes it possible to justify such regulations under that principle.

I do not wish to place great emphasis on the distinction between cooperation and good samaritan requirements. In the latter case, it is natural to think of one person's directly helping another by, say, removing him from danger or administering first aid, while in the former case one thinks of behavior within complex institutional settings or of coordination among a number of individuals, where one person's efforts could not possibly prevent the harm in question. But intermediate or mixed cases are clearly possible. For example, the coordinated efforts of a number of persons, perhaps within an institutional setting, may be needed to help a drowning, trapped, injured, or ill person. The contrast between cooperation and good samaritan requirements is useful here chiefly to suggest a variety of ways in which conduct may be regulated to prevent harm to other persons. It is not meant to suggest a sharp dichotomy or an exhaustive catalogue of cases.

It should also be emphasized that we are speaking here only of preventing harm and not of using coercion to promote benefits in general. One might object to the latter while accepting the former. Now, if one is concerned with preventing harm and believes that harm prevention may justify interference with an individuals's freedom of action, then one should regard cooperation requirements as important cases. For they may well provide the *only* means of preventing or eliminating some significant harms, such as malnutrition and starvation, emotional disturbances, illness and disease, vulnerability to attack, homelessness, and so on. In fact, it is difficult to think of major social problems that might be dealt with just by limiting conduct that causes or threatens to cause harm to others. A principle that excluded other ways of preventing or eliminating harm would restrict such efforts very seriously.

Before concluding this part of the discussion, we might consider some examples that Brown himself proposes. He says:

> There can be no guarantee that joint works necessary to the interest of society will not include institutional care for the mentally defective, urban redevelopment, or foreign aid to countries whose economic conditions might otherwise lead to war. I cannot see how refusal to co-operate in such efforts toward alleviation of existing problems could be shown to constitute causing harm to others. (p. 146).

The last remark makes clear the context of these examples: Brown is claiming that what I am calling cooperation requirements cannot be reconciled to a harmful-conduct-prevention principle, that is, to Mill's Principle of Liberty on Brown's reading of it. I grant that point. But now the question arises whether they can be reconciled to a broader harm-prevention principle. The short answer to this question is, it all depends. It is plausible to suppose that foreign aid for the purpose of preventing war could be justified on grounds of harm prevention; but other examples will depend more clearly on circumstances that are variable. To take one example: urban redevelopment, as I have seen it, in New York City and Boston, could not generally be so justified, since it is often used not to prevent or eliminate harms to others but to provide greater comforts and conveniences for relatively comfortable members of society while it actually undermines the conditions of those who are displaced and ignores their unmet basic needs.

I suggest, therefore, that the general harm-prevention version of the Principle of Liberty is more plausible than the narrower harmful conduct-prevention version. Furthermore, it appears that the former can, while the latter cannot, account for Mill's own examples.

III. Problems of Interpretation

Mill's definitive statement of his Principle of Liberty supports the general harm-prevention reading, since it predicates interference on the prevention of harm to others and does not require that it be limited to the prevention of conduct that causes harm. Mill's own examples seem to accord with a general harm-prevention principle, though they clash with the narrower harmful conduct-prevention principle attributed to Mill. Can we then conclude that (L*) is closer than (L) to Mill's evident intentions? Mill does not permit us this luxury.

Brown thinks it clear that Mill means (L) and not (L*). He says, "Mill consistently writes and argues as if he had specified, not that interference with the conduct should prevent harm to others, but rather that the conduct itself should be harmful to others." (p. 135) One cannot deny that Mill's words sometimes imply this and thus support Brown's reading. My purpose in this section is to emphasize that the evidence is equivocal.

I have already offered reasons for the general harm-prevention reading of Mill's principle. Evidence on the other side includes a number of passages which suggest the narrower harmful conduct-prevention principle. For example, in the very paragraph in which Mill gives his definitive statement, he says that, to justify threats or penalties against a person, "the conduct from which it is desired to deter him must be calculated to produce evil to someone else." [I, 9] Indeed, his use of the term "self-protection" in the general statement of the principle might be taken as suggesting the narrower reading.

But Brown's reasons for ascribing (L) rather than (L*) to Mill do not end with such evidence. They also turn upon the following line of argument. Immediately after Mill offers his cooperation and good samaritan examples, he says, "A person may cause evil to others not only by his actions but by his inaction, and in either case he is justly accountable to them for the injury." [I, 11] This suggests that Mill illicitly regards those requirements as equivalent to prohibitions against conduct that causes harm to others: if one fails to comply with them, one causes harm, not by one's act, but by one's omission, or "inaction." Brown argues that Mill would have no reason to suggest such a thing—to conflate failing to prevent harm with causing harm (by inaction)—unless he wished to assure his readers that the examples do not clash with his principle, which then must be understood to allow interference only with conduct that causes harm to others.

Brown then suggests that Mill is obliged to do this because of his other doctrinal commitments. The one emphasized by Brown is Mill's endorsement of a Principle of Enforcing Morality, which can be understood as follows:

(M) The liberty of action of the individual ought *prima facie* to be interfered with if and only if his conduct is *prima facie* morally wrong. (p. 148)

Thus, when Mill accepts a specific duty, he is committed to its enforcement. But Mill's examples represent his acceptance of "duties to help people which go beyond the avoidance of harming them." (p. 158) The result is an uncomfortable predicament for Mill, which he resolves by misdescribing his examples, imagining that they fall within the limits of his Principle of Liberty. Brown concludes that "Mill has achieved consistency at the cost of truth." (p. 133)

The attribution of (L) to Mill thus forms part of a significant systematic interpretation of Mill's doctrines, a scholarly effort to which I cannot do justice here. I must confess I have strong reservations about Brown's claim that "Mill believes in the enforcement of morality," at least as a characterization of Mill's position in *Utilitarianism*, on which Brown relies.[6] But, in any case, Brown cannot defend his reading of Mill's principle by claiming that the Principle of Enforcing Morality accounts for either Mill's examples or the predicament in which, on Brown's interpretation, Mill finds himself; nor can he claim that "Mill has achieved consistency at the cost of truth." The Principle of Enforcing Morality does not tell us what our duties are; it simply commits one who holds it to the enforcement of whatever duties we happen to have. It is therefore incapable of explaining why Mill believes that we have duties to cooperate in joint undertakings and to act as good samaritans. This is especially embarrassing for Brown's consistency claim. For, on Brown's reading, Mill is committed not just to (L) and (M), which can be understood as compatible,[7] but also to those troublesome examples. Mill's acceptance of the duties to cooperate and to be a good samaritan can be explained in either of two ways. It might rest on some further doctrine (beyond (L) and (M)) or else it might represent Mill's independent moral judgment, in which case it can be thought of as a doctrine in itself. Either way, it clashes, on Brown's account, with (L) and (M). For Mill is seen by Brown as committed (a) to certain "duties to help other people which go beyond the avoidance of harming them" and, (b) by virtue of the Principle of Enforcing Morality, to their enforcement, while (c) their enforcement is incompatible with his Principle of Liberty. On this reconstruction, Mill's position is untenable, and he cannot achieve consistency without a change of doctrine. He does not achieve consistency but merely papers over his embarrassment by misconstruing his own examples, thus sacrificing truth along with consistency. Furthermore, Brown's straightforward exposure of Mill's misdescriptions suggests that Mill exercises a considerable capacity for self-deception. These results are less generous to Mill than Brown may well intend. In any case, they should lead us to investigate alternative interpretations of Mill's doctrines.

On my account, no special explanation is required for Mill's cooperation and good samaritan examples, since they are accommodated by his Principle of Liberty. Mill faces no inconsistencies. And he endorses the most plausible principle of the type he is evidently defending.

So much for the larger questions raised by Brown's systematic reading. Let us return, now, to the most directly relevant text, Mill's own commentary on his examples. As we have seen, just after Mill presents his troublesome illustrations he observes, "A person may cause evil to others not only by his actions but also by his inaction, and in either case he is justly accountable to them for the injury." [I, 11] But this is not the end of his commentary. Brown quotes the rest, but sees no further point in it. Here is how it continues:

> The latter case, it is true, requires a much more-cautious exercise of compulsion than the former. To make anyone answerable for *doing evil* to others is the rule; to make him answerable for *not preventing evil* is, comparatively speaking, the exception. Yet there are cases clear enough and grave enough to justify that exception. [I, 11; emphasis added]

This passage shows that Mill acknowledges the very distinction that, on Brown's reading, he is supposed to neglect—between conduct that causes harm and conduct that fails to prevent harm to others. Furthermore, in employing the distinction as he does, Mill seems to be saying that he would allow interference not just to inhibit harmful conduct but also to elicit acts that prevent harm to others.

In other words, the evidence offered by this passage is equivocal. Mill's initial comment on causing evil by inaction suggests some confusion about the character of his own examples, as if he wishes to limit interference to conduct that causes harm to others. In the continuation of the passage, however, he explicitly extends interference to conduct that does not cause harm, but that fails to prevent harm, as his good samaritan examples require.

It should be observed that Mill's comments make no special allowance for cooperation requirements. From his silence on the matter, one might infer that Mill regards them as equivalent to good samaritan requirements—as if answering a subpoena were like saving a drowning person's life. That seems untenable. The failure to comply with cooperation requirements does not amount to such a simple failure to prevent harm to others. Indeed, it may have no effect at all upon harm-prevention.

Suppose that cooperation requirements are justified because they are instrumental in preventing public harms, such as social insecurity and polluted air. We can then assume that each person in the community has a stake in the effective operation of the rules and therefore in (roughly speaking) general compliance with them, that is, compliance that is sufficiently widespread to make the joint undertaking as effective as it could be. But we cannot infer from this that any single act of noncompliance places some relevant interest of some other individual at a finite and nonnegligible risk; a single act of noncompliance cannot be assumed to undermine harm-prevention efforts. It might, but then again it might not; and it is at least conceivable that one should know when a single isolated act of noncompliance will have no such consequences. Suppose, for example, that certain substances are dangerous only when they reach a critical concentration in the atmosphere. A pollution control rule might prohibit any release of such substances into the atmosphere, or it might try to reduce the frequency of such acts or the amounts of chemicals released, on the understanding that concentrations of that substance in the atmosphere below the critical level are entirely innocuous. Suppose, however, that an efficiently economical pollution control rule prohibits any release of the substance into the atmosphere, simply because it would in fact be practically impossible to administer any less rigorous rule and the upshot would be failure. It might then be the case that some particular person on at least one occasion could know that his release of a small quantity of the chemical into the atmosphere will be an isolated act of noncompliance with the rule and that the harmful concentration will never be reached. His act of noncompliance might have no effect on harm-prevention efforts and thus could not be assimilated to the failure to save a drowning man.

It must be admitted, however, that such cases may in fact be rare or even nonexistent. And, when one is reasoning about such matters probabilistically, with an eye on large-scale social engineering, there is a natural temptation to assume that we are never in a position absolutely to rule out such effects of noncompliant acts. One might then conclude that the relevant interests of each member of the community are put to some finite nonnegligible risk by any violation of the rules. If there is an error here, it should not be exaggerated. One who reasons in this way need not suppose that a single act of noncompliance causes harm to others, or even that it straightforwardly fails to prevent harm, in the way that failing to save a drowning man fails to prevent harm. He need only suppose that there is always, in such a case, some risk that harm-prevention efforts will be adversely affected. One who reasons in this way might tend to assimilate cooperation requirements to good samaritan requirements. This might help to explain why Mill fails to give separate treatment to cooperation examples.

But all of this is highly speculative and we are left, in any case, with the impression that Mill fails to appreciate the complexity of his own commitments. There is clear evidence that he wishes to allow interference not only to inhibit conduct that causes harm to others but also to elicit harm-preventing conduct, broadly construed. At the same time, there is evidence that Mill tends to back off from this commitment or else does not fully recognize the theoretical decision that he faces.

IV. Benefits and Fairness

I have accepted Brown's claim that a harmful conduct-prevention principle cannot accommodate cooperation or good samaritan requirements. Brown would, I think, agree in turn with one of my claims, namely, that good samaritan requirements can plausibly be reconciled with a general harm-prevention principle. But he appears to reject the idea that such a principle could also accommodate cooperation requirements. He says that "the general prevention of harm would not stretch to cover a fair share of every joint work necessary to the interest of society." (p. 146) He gives no defense or explanation for this assertion. One can imagine, however, why cooperation requirements might be thought incompatible with a harm-prevention principle. One reason might be the notion that such requirements are in fact predicated on promoting benefits beyond mere harm-prevention. Another concerns Mill's references to "fair shares." I will deal with these in turn.

The distinction between increasing benefits generally and merely preventing or eliminating harms is taken for granted by Mill. He assumes that some benefits would go beyond harm-prevention and thus their promotion could not serve in the justification of enforced requirements. This point requires some further explanation.

It might be assumed that Mill, as a utilitarian, should be understood in effect as following today's fashion in such matters and count the satisfaction of an existing preference as a benefit and its frustration as a harm. Mill's talk of "pleasures" and "pains" might easily suggest this. But important features of his moral and political doctrines, especially those concerning justice and liberty, seem to imply the following sort of view. While it is easy to be mistaken about what constitutes a positive benefit to another person, harms are unproblematic. Harms thus concern interests that are readily appreciated; most if not all of these are, at bottom, common to all persons. They are not to be understood in terms of mere existing preferences but rather as conditions that must be satisfied if one is to live well as a human being; they include physical necessities, personal security, social freedom (from oppressive custom as well as others' interference), and a variety of experiences and opportunities for self-development. To the extent that one is denied or deprived of such conditions, one suffers what Mill counts as "harm".

The question that we face is whether Mill's cooperation examples concern requirements that could not be justified on the basis of preventing harms (on Mill's view or any other), but could only be justified on the ground that they would increase benefits beyond harm-prevention. Mill's words imply the contrary. None of his original examples suggest that cooperation requirements may be exacted in order to obtain positive benefits, and his restatement of them later in the essay *On Liberty* implies the opposite. He says that "the fact of living in society renders it indispensable that each should observe a certain line of conduct toward the rest," which includes "each person's bearing his share (to be fixed upon some equitable principle) of the labors and sacrifices incurred for defending the society or its members from injury and molestation." [IV, 3; cf. also IV, 7] This tells us that Mill has in mind preventing harms rather than increasing benefits.

It might be noted that Mill first introduces his examples by saying that "There are also many positive acts for the benefit of others which he may rightfully be compelled to perform," which could suggest that he means "acts for the positive benefit of others" and not just acts intended to prevent harm. But this cannot be Mill's real meaning. For under the heading "positive acts for the benefit of others" he includes not only cooperation but also good samaritan requirements, and these are clearly meant to prevent harm and not to promote further benefits. Mill's words are, after all, transparent: the examples he is introducing concern requirements and thus positive acts rather than prohibitions and omissions.

Let us turn, then, to Mill's talk about "fair shares". His official doctrine is that restrictions on liberty may be imposed only for the purpose of preventing harm to others. He acknowledges that other types of reason might argue against particular restrictions, but he is unclear what they might be. The only examples he provides are these: Coercive measures might not be required or might be counter-productive either because the individuals are likely to act better on their own or the intervention would produce as side effects more harm than it would prevent. [I, 11] These particular strictures can readily be understood, since Mill is evidently committed not only to harm-prevention but also to preserving liberty, interfering with it as little as possible.[8] So, while Mill allows the definite need for some coercive intervention, he wishes to minimize it, as well as to minimize the incidental harm that social intervention entails. None of this commits Mill to considering the fairness of an enforced requirement. Fairness presumably requires that the benefits of harm-prevention and the burdens of incidental harm and loss of liberty be distributed in a certain way, according to merit or desert and respecting individual rights. Fairness could conceivably object to some rules predicated upon harm-prevention, rules that Mill would otherwise be willing to accept. We can imagine, for example, that Mill would be prepared to endorse the least burdensome rule among a set of equally effective alternatives, that is, the one that prevents a given harm or set of harms at a minimal loss of liberty and a minimal cost in incidental harms. At the same time, we can imagine that such a rule would be condemned by fairness on the ground that it does not distribute benefits and burdens equitably. Mill's references in his cooperation examples to considerations of fairness would seem, then, to commit him to rejecting such minimally burdensome but effective rules in favor of rules with greater social costs or more extensive limitations on liberty.

Such an abstract, theoretical possibility cannot be denied. But I think the potential problems here might easily be exaggerated. Compare the argument that utilitarianism is defective because it requires that benefits be maximized (and burdens minimized) and thus ignores considerations of justice, which concern their distribution. It is sometimes said, for example, that slavery, which involves the unjust exploitation of some for the sake of others' benefits, might be justified on utilitarian grounds, which shows that utilitarianism is defective. This is, I think, in many ways a highly questionable argument against utilitarianism. But my point just now is that some relevant features of this purely abstract argument against utilitarianism are not available in the cases we must consider with regard to fairness and harm-prevention. The Principle of Liberty permits some "trade-offs," but it never sanctions the imposition of burdens on some for the sake of others' positive benefits. No benefits beyond harm-prevention can justify coercion under the Principle of Liberty. The trade-offs it allows are these: loss of liberty (plus some incidental harm by way of side effects or social costs of enforcement) in order to prevent or eliminate greater harm to others. Details of distribution aside, this is a morally respectable position.

The potential problems might be exaggerated in other ways too. An example will help to show this. Mill is concerned specifically with rules that impose requirements such as giving testimony in court or providing some form of public service. Let us take the familiar example of military service, which he suggests. Suppose a society must mobilize a military force in order to defend itself against unwarranted attack. Harm-prevention dictates that the mobilization be effective: it must be adequate to secure the community against attack. And it presumably wishes to minimize the harm and loss of liberty that may be required for that purpose. Fairness requires that the burdens be distributed in a certain way. It is worth noting that fairness does not argue, all by itself, for the basic restriction in such a case: it simply sets limits on the means used to achieve other legitimate purposes. It has no objection to minimizing harm and loss of liberty, other things being equal, and it would not require that burdens be imposed when they would not be at all effective in achieving the basic harm-prevention project. For simplicity's sake, let us make some assumptions that will not affect the main point of this example. Let us assume that the persons selected by fairness to shoulder the burdens of military service are capable of achieving the harm-prevention objective; that the only relevant burdens are military service; that these burdens fall equally heavily upon anyone who shoulders them; that the benefit is security from attack, which all stand to receive; and that all members of the community are equally capable of performing the required service. Now, fairness requires either that these burdens fall on some particular members of the community (because they owe such service to others, let us say, or the others have the right to be excused from service) or it does not. In either case, there are two possibilities: either the class picked out as eligible for military service contains just enough members for that purpose, so that all must serve, or it contains more than enough, so that some might be excused if loss of liberty and other social costs are to be minimized. If the eligible class contains just enough members for the purpose, then there is no conflict between fairness and harm-prevention, since fairness does not require any restrictions upon liberty that could not be justified on harm-prevention grounds alone. If the class contains more than enough members, then I assume that fairness would not object to minimizing burdens by excusing some in a fair (e.g., random) manner, such as a lottery. In this case, too, then, fairness would not conflict with harm-prevention.

I do not mean that there is no difference between the two criteria, that they must inevitably approve of just the same rules for harm-prevention. Clearly, we have been assuming, on the contrary, that harm-prevention can accept some assignments of burdens that are unfairly made. Suppose, for example, that only a portion of the community is required for military service. Fairness might require that those who have not served before, in such a situation, should be chosen first, while harm-prevention would, other things being equal, be indifferent to which members are chosen, so long as enough are mobilized and not too many. This is agreed. My point is, rather, that many arguments from fairness do not require extra burdens, beyond those that could be justified on harm-prevention grounds; they require only certain distributions of those burdens. Whenever burdens can be minimized without affecting harm-prevention efforts, fairness would approve so long as the results are achieved in accordance with some fair procedure. To this extent, arguments from fairness do not function as reasons for imposing restrictions. They accordingly appear compatible with Mill's Principle of Liberty, which only requires economical harm-prevention. And to this degree, at least, it seems reasonable to conclude that cooperation limited by fairness is compatible with the Principle of Liberty and thus that Mill's examples might present no difficulties for him.

If considerations of fairness are to present a more substantial threat either to Mill's principle or to his examples, there must be cases in which they object, in effect, to minimizing burdens in the course of harm-prevention. For, if they do, then they might be regarded as functioning as independent reasons for coercive intervention, and therefore as conflicting with the Principle of Liberty.

I do not believe that Mill regards them in that way. He discusses justice in *Utilitarianism*, and he says there that "Justice is a name for certain classes of moral rules which concern the essentials of human well-being more nearly, and are therefore of more absolute obligation, than any other rules for the guidance of life."[9] Mill plainly believes that injustice and unfairness threaten the most vital of human interests, and that the protection of those interests is the rationale behind the corresponding principles. He thus regards considerations of justice and fairness as rooted in, not as independent of, harm-prevention. More important, Mill understands these principles as exerting independent weight in moral reasoning, relative to welfare arguments.

On the usual reading of Mill, he is understood to hold that we are always morally bound to promote the general welfare—that any other way of acting is fundamentally wrong. He acknowledges that we require guidance from some "secondary" rules, based on past experience concerning the most reliable ways of promoting welfare. Mill's appeal to considerations of fairness, then, would be understood as an appeal to a particular collection of rules of thumb, rules that specifically concern certain fundamental human interests, but which are to be followed because experience counsels adherence to them, as the best way of promoting welfare. On my reading of Mill, however, this is a caricature of his approach to morality and justice.[10]

Mill asserts, as a conceptual claim, that morality concerns moral rights and obligations. Moral principles lay down obligations; the principles of justice lay down obligations that correlate with others' personal rights. To be moral is to perform our obligations; to be just is to respect others' rights. To be just, then, one must reject rules that violate others' rights. Mill recognizes no general "obligation" to "maximize utility"; considerations of the general welfare do not enter directly into moral reasoning. Mill believes, of course, that welfare considerations provide the only sound basis for moral principles. But adherence to such principles is not equivalent or reducible to maximizing utility. The principles of justice are predicated on protecting the vital interests of human beings, such as personal security and freedom from others' intervention. They are based on large scale, long term arguments about those interests. These arguments yield principles, such as the Principle of Liberty itself, which lay down rights and obligations that must be respected (save when they are overridden by other moral rights or obligations). In this respect, Mill may be said to "take rights seriously": for they exert independent weight in moral argument; mere welfare arguments cannot override them. Such rights are consequently capable of conflicting with, and overruling, arguments based on harm-prevention alone. Equally effective and economical restrictions could be distinguished by Mill on the basis of the principles of justice. If any rules predicated simply upon harm-prevention would violate moral rights, they must be rejected. Thus fairness could, in Mill's view, be rooted in harm-prevention and still serve, in effect, as an independent condition to be satisfied by morally acceptable restrictions.

Mill's Principle of Liberty must be understood accordingly. One of the reasons that Mill must recognize as vetoing a harm-prevention rule is that it violates moral rights. This reconciles Mill to the idea of accepting rules that impose more than the minimal burdens required for harm-prevention alone, if such rules should be entertained. But this qualification on the Principle of Liberty is itself predicated upon the protection of certain vital human interests, or in other words upon the prevention of harm to others.

Mill's view will not satisfy the critics of utilitarianism who maintain that justice and fairness are independent of utility. They may be right. I have only sketched the sort of view suggested by Mill and described how it might overcome some fundamental obstacles to a utilitarian account of justice. But the adequacy of such an account has no more been established than the contrary.

All of this is, however, beside the point, if we are primarily concerned with Mill's doctrine of liberty. His utilitarian account of
justice, while relevant to an understanding of his cooperation
examples and the Principle of Liberty itself, is not entailed by the
Principle of Liberty. Thus, even if one believes that justice is independent of utility, one might wish to consider whether Mill is
nonetheless on the right track about liberty and harm to others.
For it is not obvious—though it seems often to be assumed—that
considerations of justice and fairness, all by themselves, not only
help to determine what conduct is right and wrong but also justify
measures of coercion. One might question this. One who rejected
Mill's account of justice might consistently accept his Principle of
Liberty. One might find reason to agree that considerations of fairness alone never justify coercion, that only harm-prevention does.

Notes

1. Work on this paper was supported by a fellowship from the National
Endowment for the Humanities, which I am happy to acknowledge. Earlier versions
were read at the University of Calgary, Simon Fraser University, and the University of
Washington, where I received many helpful comments. I am especially grateful to
Jonathan Bennett, D. G. Brown, David Copp, Samuel Scheffler, and Barry Smith for
criticisms.
   2. All references in brackets are to chapters and paragraphs of John Stuart Mill, *On
Liberty* (first published 1859).
   3. D. G. Brown, "Mill on Liberty and Morality," *Philosophical Review*, 81 (1972),
133–158.
   4. All page references within parentheses are to the article by Brown, *ibid.*
   5. Or at least dangerous; cf. *ibid.*, p. 135, n. 2.
   6. The relevant passage is *Utilitarianism*, Chapter V, paragraph 14. For my interpretation, see "Mill's Theory of Morality," *Noûs*, 10 (1976), 101–120.
   7. Since the Principle of Liberty purports to tell us the sole valid ground for coercive intervention, the Principle of Enforcing Morality must be understood to say, not
that immorality is itself a justification for interference, but rather that there is some
such justification whenever conduct is wrong. It is therefore somewhat misleading for
Brown to say (p. 146) that "Mill believes in the enforcement of morality."
   8. Cf. Brown, pp. 137–139.
   9. *Utilitarianism*, Chapter V, paragraph 32.
   10. I discuss this further in "Human Rights and the General Welfare," *Philosophy &
Public Affairs*, 6 (1977), 113–129, and also in "Mill's Theory of Justice," in *Values and
Morals: Essays in Honor of William Frankena, Charles Stevenson, and Richard Brandt*, ed. A.
I. Goldman and J. Kim, (Dordrecht: Reidel, 1978), 1–20.

7

Profound Offense

Joel Feinberg

1. Limits to the Nuisance Model

If the full gravamen of the wrong in all offensive conduct is mere nuisance—harmless annoyance, unpleasantness, and inconvenience—then it is quite impossible to understand why the criminal law, rightly or wrongly, has taken offensiveness so seriously in the past. The very word "nuisance" suggests something relatively trivial, hardly a term to do justice to the profound feelings of righteous abhorrence that certain practices evoke in persons of ordinary sensitivity, even when those practices are believed to be, by and large, harmless and unobtrusive. Nuisance may be a matter of small importance for the criminal law, but there are some forms of offensiveness that are taken so seriously that some have advocated severe punishment for them even when they are not, strictly speaking, nuisances.

It will be useful to reserve the term "nuisance" for the miscellany of unpleasant states discussed in Chapters 7 and 8 when they are imposed upon someone in circumstances that make them difficult to avoid or escape. Nuisances so conceived are annoyances or inconveniences, and when they are believed to be caused wrongfully, they are resented ("taken offense at"), and thus become offenses in a strict and narrow sense. When they are in fact unjustified, as determined by the balancing tests of Chapter 8, that is a reason for legally prohibiting the conduct that produces them. Some of the offended states of mind in the broad miscellany have a felt character that seems to mark them off from all the others and for which the term "nuisance" seems too pallid even when they are not difficult to avoid or escape without annoying inconvenience. Sometimes, to be sure, these *profound offenses* are produced in circumstances (like those of the bus ride in Chapter 7) that make them impossible to avoid witnessing and add an extra dimension of annoyance and inconvenience to them. But unlike the other offensive nuisances, these profound ones would continue to rankle even when unwitnessed, and they would thus be offensive even when they are not, strictly speaking, nuisances at all. On the other side, those inescapable unpleasant experiences that are contrasted with the "profound" ones we can call *offensive nuisances merely*. Lacking the felt "profound" character of the others, they can be called "mere nuisances" without trivializing understatement, and we can plausibly claim legal protection from them only in circumstances in which they *are* indefensible intrusions (difficult to escape and unjustified by the balancing tests), and then only because they are such nuisances. Not all of the offensive actions on the bus ride in Chapter 7 are "offensive nuisances merely," though surely most are. The affronts to the senses clearly are of this kind, as are the disgusting indulgences and embarrassing indecencies. The religious caricatures and ethnic insults, however, while also "nuisances" in the situation (that is, they are annoying and inescapable), are somehow *that and more*, so that "nuisance" seems an understatement, and their evil seems independent of its unavoidability (in the strict sense that word bears in the balancing tests). Some might wish to criminalize the acts that knowingly produce these "profound offenses" even when they do not fully satisfy the balancing tests that are modelled after nuisance law. I think I understand the motives of these people, but I will try to rebut their arguments here.

Before listing the defining characteristics of "offensive nuisances merely" and "profound offenses," it would be wise to examine some putative examples of the latter. Profound offenses are disconcertingly diverse, but perhaps the following are representative.

1. *Voyeurism*. In 1983 the CBS television news show "Sixty Minutes" told the story of some women employees of a Kentucky coal mining company. The women had won employment as miners, a job hitherto reserved for men, and for several years they had discharged their duties competently and faithfully. But they had never been fully accepted by many of the male miners. One day they discovered to their horror that there were peepholes bored through a wall that separated a supply room to which the men had access from the women's shower room and lavatory. To say that the women "took offense" at this discovery or "suffered annoyance" is grossly inadequate. Both the women and their lawyer spoke passionately of the victims' embarrassment, mortification, humiliation, and of the affront to their dignity. Their chagrin was so severe that it probably had genuinely harmful effects on most of them, perhaps setbacks to a genuine "interest in personal privacy," or a permanent damaging of their relations with their fellow workers, or debilitating depression, sleeplessness, and anguish; but even in the possible cases where the threshold of actual harm had not been reached, a serious wrong was surely done them. The feelings of mortification and the like were no less powerful for being retroactive, and the description that characterizes the evil they suffered as "unpleasant states of mind" even of great intensity and durability (the language of nuisance) seems to miss a qualitative difference from ordinary offensive nuisances. The example is an impressive and pertinent one even though criminal prohibitions of the offending behavior would probably be legitimized anyway by both the harm principle and the offense principle as mediated by the balancing tests proposed in Chapter 8. (The women chose to sue for civil damages, and settled out of court for an undisclosed payment and a public apology.)

2. *Nazis and klansmen*. The feelings of an aged Jewish survivor of a Nazi death camp as a small band of American Nazis strut in full regalia down the main street of his or her town, or those of some American blacks as robed Ku Klux Klan members hold a demonstration in the public square of their town, have several relevant components that help to mark them off from ordinary offensive

nuisances. First, the feelings cannot be wholly escaped merely by withdrawing one's attention, by locking one's door, pulling the window blinds, and putting plugs in one's ears. The offended state of mind is at least to some degree independent of what is directly perceived. Second, there is an element of direct personal danger and threat to others whom one holds dear. The demonstrators, after all, are affiliated by their own design with the very groups that have murdered millions of Jews and tormented and lynched countless blacks in the past. Third, and more importantly, the hated symbols of the demonstrators are affronts to something the offended parties hold dear and, like the memory of their dead kinsmen, even sacred.

3. *Execrated but "harmless" deviant religious and moral practices.* A religious practice or moral conviction may be just as "dear" or "sacred" to a totally committed person as the memory of murdered kinsmen is to the Jew or the black, and cults or practices thought to be heretical or deviant judged to be as abominable and loathsome as the Nazi parades and Klan demonstrations. Thus Robert Paul Wolff claims that to a devout Calvinist or a principled vegetarian "the very presence in his community of a Catholic or a meat-eater may cause him fully as much pain as a blow to the face or a theft of his purse" and speaks of "the presence of ungodly persons in [the] community" as "torturing [one's] soul" and "destroying [one's] sleep."[1] Note that Wolff refers only to the "presence in the community" of religiously or morally deviant persons even when they are withdrawn, private, and discreet, unlike the arrogant demonstrators of the previous example. Lest this hypothetical example seem too extreme, the reader should be reminded that for centuries Protestant churches were illegal in Catholic Spain, that the "private" slaughtering of beef cattle is illegal in India, raising hogs commercially is forbidden to Israelis, and the celebration of the mass and the wearing of Christian clerical garb even by foreigners and in private are criminal offenses in Saudi Arabia, where they are thought to be stenches in the nostrils of God. Of course such criminal prohibitions cannot be legitimized either by the harm principle, or the offense principle as

applied to ordinary offensive nuisances through the balancing tests. If religious rites and private dining customs were prohibited on such grounds, no one could ever feel secure in his liberty so longer as "devout and principled persons" are filled with loathing at the very thought of what he does in private. (Where different devout and principled groups loathe one another equally, a situation not unknown to history, a prohibitive criminal law aimed at the practices of either could only lead to civil strife.) But if we advocate relaxing the balancing tests for the application of the offense principle in the case of profound offenses like those of the Jews and the blacks in the earlier example, we shall have to find a way of distinguishing that kind of case from the present one. The profoundly offended states of mind in the two kinds of example may *feel* very much alike.

4. *Venerated symbols.* Traditionally, criminal codes have contained provisions outlawing defacing the national flag or other objects of public veneration, and mistreating corpses. Since flags, crucifixes, and dead bodies are not the sorts of objects that have interests of their own, they cannot be "harmed" in the sense of the harm principle. (See Vol. I, Chap. 1, §1.) When these profoundly offensive acts are done in public they can be considered public nuisances and punished accordingly, though when they are interpreted as expressions of dissent, or "private expression of political disaffection,"[2] it is doubtful that they would be certified as wrongful by any balancing test that gives great importance to the value of political expression. But when these acts are done discreetly in private they are more surely unreachable by any plausible balancing test that gives preemptive weight to reasonable avoidability. Indeed, since they are easily avoidable by everyone, they are not even properly called "nuisances" in the first place. And yet state penal codes have commonly prohibited such acts in the past, no doubt because of the qualitatively unique, "profound" character of the offense they produce in the bare contemplation. In Pennsylvania, for example, a 1945 statute provides punishment for anyone who "publicly *or privately* mutilates, defaces, defiles, or tramples

upon, or casts contempt either by words or acts upon any such flag."[3]

There is no doubt that widespread and profound offense would be taken at an atheist group that held regular private, but open-to-the-public meetings, in its own anti-church building, at which they defaced prints of religious paintings, obscenely decorated religious icons, set fire to sacred texts, and so on. Modern blasphemy and sacrilege statutes penalize, for the most part, only "the mischievous or zealous blasphemer who purposely disrupts a religious meeting or procession with utterances designed to outrage the sensibilities of the group and thus provoke a riot."[4] But in other times and places, the privately meeting atheists would not have been so fortunate, and the penalties of the law would have been imposed on them if only because of the peculiarly deep character of the offense they produced to the religious sensibility. It is worth noting that a sense of fairness has never impelled a legislature to penalize clergymen and their congregations for savage denunciations in their churches of law-abiding atheists. The point is not, or is not simply, that the lawmaker's sense of reciprocity was deficient, but rather that the resentment of the atheists at the mockery of their beliefs does not constitute *profound* offense, since nothing they hold sacred is impugned by it.

There is also widespread and profound offense taken at the defilement of the ultimate symbol of love of country, the national flag under whose banners generations of heroes have fought and died. And even more profound feelings are aroused by the mistreatment of dead bodies. The authors of the *Model Penal Code* struggled with the question of whether offenses of these two kinds are profound enough to warrant punishment even of the private performance of the acts that cause them. The outcome was a compromise. "Section 250.10 penalizes mistreatment of a corpse 'in a way that [the actor] . . . knows would outrage ordinary family sensibilities', although the actor may have taken every precaution for secrecy . . . On the other hand, desecration of the national flag or other object of public veneration, an offense under Section 250.9, is not committed unless others are likely to "observe or discover'."[5] Why should there be this difference? One of the chief authors of the Code, Louis Schwartz, explains it as follows:

> As I search for the principle of discrimination between the morals offenses made punishable only when committed openly and those punishable even when committed in secrecy, I find nothing but differences in the intensity of the aversion with which the different kinds of behavior are regarded. It was the intuition of the drafts-man and his fellow lawmakers at the Institute that disrespectful behavior to a corpse [is a] more intolerable affront to ordinary feel-ings than disrespectful behavior to a flag. Therefore, in the former case but not the latter, we overcame our general reluctance to extend penal controls . . . to private behavior that disquiets people solely because they learn that things of this sort are going on.[6]

It accords with my "intuition" too that most people would find mistreatment of dead bodies a "more intolerable affront" to their feelings than desecration of a flag, but this does not imply neces-sarily that the "intensity of their aversion" in the dead body case is greater than in the flag case. If intensity were the relevant cri-terion of comparison, then deferring to "ordinary feelings" of the public at large, we might well criminalize coprophagia, the eat-ing of live worms, anal intercourse, even scratching fingernails on slate and going bathless for weeks at a time, "although the actors may have taken every precaution for secrecy". The more likely explanation is that though the offended reactions in both the flag and dead body cases are qualitatively different from other kinds of offense, in that they are both affronts to the higher-order sensi-bilities (See Chap. 7, § 4), they also differ from one another in that the moral principle affronted symbolically by mistreatment of corpses—respect for humanity—is more fundamental than the moral principle symbolically affronted by flag desecration, namely fidelity to country. The offense taken at the mistreatment of corpses then might be still more "profound," questions of intensity and duration of aversion aside.

There is another difference between dead bodies and flags that may have some bearing on the difference in our reactions to their respective mutilations. A flag is an arbitrary or conventional symbol of an abstraction, which bears no striking similarity to what it symbolizes. Rather it comes to represent a country only by virtue of a conventional understanding. If someone designed an entirely different flag, say one that featured green geometrical abstractions on a field of gold and black stripes, and we all agreed to adopt the new emblem, then it would come to represent the United States, though its colors and shapes are no less arbitrary than those of the symbol it replaced. A dead body, on the other hand, is a natural symbol of a living person, and needless to say has a striking similarity to the real thing. When one mutilates a corpse one is doing something that *looks* very much like mutilating a real person, and the spontaneous horror of the real crime spills over on the symbolic one. Schwartz makes a different but closely related point when he writes: "I submit that legislative tolerance for private flag desecration is explicable by the greater difficulty an ordinary [person] has in identifying with a country and all else that a flag symbolizes as compared with the ease in identifying with a corpse . . ."[7] There is a point to this observation. If I saw a stranger on the bus open a coffin and pound the face of the newly dead person inside of it with a hammer (Chap. 7, §3), my reaction would be to move my hand to my own face, and wince as if I were the one who had been struck. My reaction to the desecration of a flag would be nothing like that. Imaginative projection of self into the mistreated object, however, while significant, only helps to explain the greater intensity of the aversion, not the degree of impact on moral sensibility, the factor that makes an offense "profound".

5. *Abortion and the mistreatment of corpses.* Some opponents of abortion think of the human fetus from the moment of conception as a living person with interests and rights, chief of which are the interest in staying alive and the corresponding "right to life". According to this view, when one deliberately kills the fetus at any stage of its development one violates that right and defeats the corresponding interest, thus wronging and harming (in the sense of the harm principle) the "victim". Many other persons, including some who are opposed to abortion for other reasons, find it insurmountably difficult to think of a fetus, especially in

its earlier stages (and *a fortiori* when it is a mere fertilized egg) as an actual person, since it lacks many of the characteristics that a person has: more than rudimentary consciousness, understanding, possession of a concept and awareness of oneself.[8] The fetus possesses these characteristics *potentially*, of course, but that shows only that the fetus is a potential person, not that it is an actual one already possessed of interests and rights.

Still, from as early as the tenth week the fetus has a recognizably human face and chubby little human hands. If only we could see it then, we would be struck by its physical resemblance to a little baby. Zealous opponents of legalized abortion take advantage of that resemblance to push their case. Many of them carry photographs of cute and lovable ten-week-old "unborn babies", and descriptions of the violence normal methods of surgical abortion impose on them. It is hard not to recoil at the very thought of their forceful destruction. Yet that does not prove that ten-week-old fetuses are right-bearing persons. One can still deny with unshaken confidence that they have a right to life, since having recognizably human features and the capacity to evoke tender responses from observers are not plausible criteria of personhood. The strongest inference we can make from the impact of the photograph on our sentiments is that there may be morally relevant properties of fetuses other than rights and personhood that have a bearing on how we ought to treat them (though not necessarily on any question of the propriety of legal coercion.) In particular, what is suggested to me is that ten-week-old fetuses, by virtue of their recognizably human features, are natural symbols, themselves only prepersons, yet as such sacred symbols of the real thing. As symbols they become the objects of transferred tender sentiments, and their destruction might understandably shock some persons in the manner of a violent desecration of any cherished icon, causing profound offense indeed.

The question of the relevance of profound offense arises even more clearly in a class of issues to be treated below (§ 5) involving the treatment of corpses. A newly dead human body is even more natural a symbol of a human person than is a developing fetus. Both postpersons and prepersons are naturally associated with actual persons, and thus become natural repositories for the sentiments real persons evoke in us, but our sentiments are even more sharply focused on the neomort because it is not only a symbol of human beings generally, but unlike the fetus, it is the symbolic remains of a particular person and his specific traits and history. Moreover, we are not even tempted in rhetoric to ascribe rights and interests to the neomort (with the possible exception of those stemming from testimonial directions he left before he died), and surely not "the right to life." One cannot murder a corpse, or commit assault or battery or rape on it; but one can violate it symbolically, and few societies are prepared to tolerate its public mutilation. Hacking it up and throwing its limbs about would be, as we say, a shock to decent human sentiment.

If any *rights* at all are violated by such treatment, it must be the rights of captive spectators not to suffer offense, and of other third parties not to suffer profound offense even at what they do not witness. But the conduct might be wrong without violating anyone's rights at all.

2. The Distinctive Characteristics of Profound Offense

Now that we have some examples of profound offenses in mind, how can we summarize their differences from what we have called "offensive nuisances merely"? Let us begin by enumerating the features generally characteristic of the offended states in mere offensive nuisance. These experiences are, first of all, relatively trivial or shallow, not only compared to harms but also compared to some other mental states, for example those that result from offense to higher-order sensibilities. Second, the wrong in mere offensive nuisance coincides with the perceptual experience that is imposed on the victim and its caused aftereffects, and is inseparable from those experiences. Without the direct perception of the offending conduct, there would be no offense, even if the person learned secondhand that the offending conduct would occur or had occurred. It is experiencing the conduct, not merely knowing about it, that offends. In respect to a mere offensive nuisance, its *esse est percipii* (its being consists in its being perceived). Third, the offense in ordinary offensive nuisance is experienced in all cases as at least partly *personal*, and in most cases as wholly personal. The offended party thinks of *himself* as the wronged victim of the conduct that causes him to have certain unpleasant and inescapable states of mind. Being disgusted, revolted, shocked, frightened, angered, bored, embarrassed, shamed, or made anxious, are like being hurt in that one has a grievance in one's own name, on one's own behalf, against the offender for making one undergo the experience. And if one had not been present, one could have had no such complaint. Fourth, it is generally characteristic of the wrong in mere offensive nuisances that it derives from an affront to one's senses, or to one's lower order sensibilities (see Chap. 7, §4.) One does not think of the offending conduct as the sort that would be wrong (in contravention of one's own standards) wherever it might occur, but wrong only because it occurs here and now, thus victimizing its reluctant witnesses. In language suggested by Kurt Baier,[9] the conduct affronts our sensibility without necessarily violating any of our *standards* of sensibility or propriety. It can therefore "offend our senses" (or lower order sensibilities) without offending *us*. Fifth and finally, in ordinary offensive nuisances the offending behavior is thought wrong (and hence resented, and hence an "offense" in the strict and narrow sense) because it produces unpleasant states in the captive witnesses, not the other way around. It does not produce unpleasant states because it is thought wrong on independent grounds.[10]

The characteristics of profound offense contrast with those of the ordinary nuisances in all five respects. First, they have an inexpressibly different felt "tone", best approximated by saying that they are deep, profound, shattering, serious, even more likely to cause harm by their obsessiveness to those who experience them. That is why the word "nuisance", with its unavoidable suggestions of triviality, is inadequate. Second, even when one does not perceive the offending conduct directly, one can be offended "at the very idea" of that sort of thing happening even in private.

A nude person on the public bus may be an offense in my sight, but I am not offended at the very idea of that person being nude in the privacy of his or her own rooms, which is to say that my offense is not of the profound kind. Some of the examples of disgusting conduct (mere offensive nuisance) may seem different in this respect. I am disgusted by the sight of the bus passengers eating vomit, and at first it might seem that I am almost as offended by the very thought of them doing so in the privacy of their own dining rooms. But in fact my offense at what is not present seems to grow only as I succeed in forming a precise image—visual, auditory, and olfactory—in my imagination, in which case it is not that a standard of propriety is violated by the very idea of certain conduct; rather an offense is produced by my own energetic image-making. *I* am the party in that case who produces an offensive experience in myself, and I can have a grievance only against myself. It is as if by intense concentration I form a precise image of the bus passenger naked in his or her own bedroom, focus all of my attention on it, and then complain that that person "profoundly offends" me by his or her habitual unwitnessed nudity. My offense at the very idea of certain conduct is not profound because I *would* be offended by that conduct if I were to witness it; rather it is profound because I am offended by its taking place at all whether I witness it or not. On the other hand, if it were possible for a person to have the strange basic moral conviction that even private nudity is sinful because (say) it is an embarrassment to God,[11] then the offense such a person feels at others being naked in their own homes every night would indeed be of the "profound" variety.

Third, in the case of profound offense, even when the evil *is* in the perceiving, something offends *us* and not merely our senses or lower order sensibilities. Our reaction is not like that of the man in the proverbial tale who, unable to bear the sight of a lady standing in the bus, always averted his eyes (rather than offer his seat) when confronted with the prospect. Profound offense cannot be avoided by averting one's eyes. Fourth, because profound offense results from an affront to the standards of propriety that determine one's higher-order sensibilities, it offends because it is believed wrong, not the other way round. It is not believed to be wrong simply and entirely because it causes offense.

Finally, profound offenses in all cases are experienced as at least partly *impersonal*, and in most cases as entirely impersonal. The offended party does not think of *himself* as the victim in unwitnessed flag defacings, corpse mutilations, religious icon desecrations, or abortions, and he does not therefore feel aggrieved (wronged) on his own behalf. The peeping-Tom and racial insult cases are, of course, exceptions to this. Here we should say that there is a merging of the two kinds of offense. The victim's outrage is profound because it is caused by a shocking affront to his or her deepest moral sensibilities, but he or she also happens to be the violated or threatened victim of the affronting behavior. In contrast, in the flag, icon, dead body, and abortion cases, there is no person at all in whose name to voice a complaint, except the profoundly offended party, and the only thing he could complain about in his own behalf is his offended state of mind. But *that* is not what he is offended at.

Still, in the confusion of strong feelings of different kinds, people are likely to mistake what it is they are indignant about. Mill reminds us that "There are many who consider as an injury to themselves any conduct which they have a distaste for [witnessed or not], and resent it as an outrage to their feelings . . ."[12] These people might be those whose profound offense at the reported private conduct of others is taken on behalf of an impersonal principle, or sacred symbol, or the like. Then coming to resent their own unpleasant state of mind as a nuisance (even though its character as felt annoyance was originally an insignificant component in what was experienced), they refocus their grievance, putting themselves in the forefront as "injured" parties. When they take this further step, however, their grievance—originally impersonal but now voiced in their own behalf—loses almost all its moral force. Mill's response to them is devastating:

> . . . as a religious bigot, when charged with disregarding the religious feelings of others, has been known to retort that they disregard his feelings by persisting in their abominable worship or

creed. But there is no parity between the feeling of a person for his own opinion and the feeling of another who is offended at his holding it, no more than between the desire of a thief to take a purse and the desire of the right owner to keep it. And a person's taste is as much his own peculiar concern as his opinion or his purse.[13]

Takers of profound offense at unwitnessed conduct are better advised to rest their claim for "protection" on impersonal grounds.

In the voyeurism and racial insult cases the primary offended parties are the direct intended targets of the behavior that does the offending, and their offense is profound because what they feel to be violated or affronted is something they hold precious (human dignity, solidarity with martyred kinsmen). Their reaction *of course* is more than mere "annoyance," and for that reason, among others, we call it "profound". In the other cases, the offense is taken on behalf of something external to oneself, and the offense is profound because of its powerful impact on one's moral sensibilities, even in the absense of any strong feeling of personal involvement. Indeed, as the feeling of aggrieved personal nuisance becomes stronger, the impersonal shock and outrage necessarily becomes weaker, and the whole experience begins to lose its profound character. When the offended reaction to a reported private mutilation of a dead body (say) is genuinely profound in the sense developed here, the offended party is not thinking of himself at all. He is involved in the offended state simply as its subject, not as part of its subject matter.

3. The Bare Knowledge Problem Again

The notion of profound offense leads us to take more seriously a question we earlier treated somewhat dismissively (see Chap. 8, §1). The "bare knowledge" problem calls for a decision about how the offense principle is to be applied. When it is the prevention of offense to which legislators appeal for the legitimization of a proposed statute, *whose* offense may appropriately be considered? (1) That of all observers? Clearly not, for those who voluntarily assumed the risk of offense have no complaint, and those who can escape it easily have hardly any more complaint. Shall we say then that (2) all and only *captive* observers should be considered? Or should we weigh also (3) the offense of non-observers who are affected by the "bare knowledge" that the offending acts are taking place in a known location beyond their observations? Perhaps we should go even further and consider (4) the offense of anyone with the very bare knowledge that when such acts are legal they *might* be taking place somewhere—almost anywhere at all—for all one knows, and with perfect impunity at that? If we draw the line to include (3) and exclude (4), then those who practice their pro-foundly offensive vices silently and discreetly behind locked doors and drawn blinds would escape the clutches of the law because they do not offend any *observers* and, since no non-observer can *know* what takes place in their rooms, no one can be offended by the bare thought that flag-defacing, homosexual lovemaking, or the like is going on there. But those who behave in unobserved privacy but make no effort to conceal from others what they are doing, may indeed offend some non-observers who suffer from their bare knowledge, and these offenders could even incur criminal liability if the sensibilities of the people in group (3) are included.

Kurt Baier has made this point with his usual clarity:

> . . . where there are standards that are widely and deeply embed-ded, witnessing is not necessary to cause offense. Of course, if I draw the blinds whenever I eat human flesh for dinner or have sexual intercourse with my goat or with my devoted sister, then no one's sensibilities can be affronted by witnessing what I am doing. But if I tell others or invite them to parties and ask them to bring their own favorite corpse or goat or relative, the case is different. The fact that they need not come or participate is not necessarily sufficient to make my behavior inoffensive . . . A neon sign on my house proclaiming *"Cannibalism, Bestiality, Incest. Tickets $5.00. Meals $25. Close relatives half price"* would be even more offensive to those who accept the relevant standards of sensibility.[14]

If we permit the activities in Baier's examples, but prohibit the participants from describing their activities to others, inviting others to join them, or soliciting through public announcement or advertising, then we have respected their liberty to act as they wish in private at the cost of their liberties to speak, write, communicate, or express themselves as they wish (one of their basic rights). On the balancing scales, by virtue of the great weight of free expression as both a personal and public good, the case against forbidding the expressive behavior might be even stronger than the case against criminalizing the primary offensive conduct.

The American Law Institute was indeed tempted to recommend, in its *Model Penal Code*, that profoundly offensive but harmless conduct be permitted in private but only when the participants have made reasonable efforts to be discreet and preserve the secrecy of their activities. Those who recommended this approach suggested the use of a familiar phrase in Anglo-American criminal statutes for the sort of behavior they would penalize: *open and notorious* illicit relations, as opposed to discreet and unflaunted ones, would be made criminal. Louis B. Schwartz tells us that the Institute finally rejected this suggestion on the ground that it is unwise to establish a penal offense in which "guilt would depend on the level of gossip to which the moral transgression gave rise."[15] I am not sure exactly what this means, but I can imagine that the code-makers had in mind such a scenario as the following. Two "profound offenders" (homosexual lovers, flag defacers, corpse mutilators, whatever) rent a flat for the purpose of secretly engaging in their odious practice at regular times and intervals. At first, no one in the neighborhood knows or cares. After a time, however, their landlady, overcome with curiosity, peeps in the keyhole, and is duly scandalized. Being a compulsive gossiper, she quickly spreads the word all over the neighborhood. In time groups of children form the habit of waiting for the couple to arrive and following them, jeering and taunting, all the way to their door, while grown-ups stand on the fringes of the excitement, gathered in animated gossiping groups. Inevitably the comings and goings of the scandalous couple become a kind of public spectacle, and everyone knows exactly what they are doing, and where and when they do it, despite their best efforts at concealment. In time their activities, even though unwitnessed, become a "flagrant affront" to the whole community, and the offense principle, extended to protect the sensibilities of those in group (3), justifies their arrest and criminal conviction. Surely criminal liability, the code-makers seem to be saying, ought not to rest on one's bad luck in finding a gossipy landlady. Either those who are lucky in keeping their secret ought *also* to be punished [in virtue of their offense to those with "very bare knowledge" in group (4)] or neither the lucky nor the unlucky ones should be punished despite the offense to those in group (3). To treat the two groups differently would be to let their guilt "depend on the level of gossip" reached through causes beyond their control. But that would still leave a third group—Baier's unrepentent indiscreet offenders, whose offending actions are done in private, but who take no steps to keep their existence unknown to others. The argument against penalizing *them*, as we have seen, is that interference with free expression can be justified by the balancing tests only when there is an enormous weight on the opposite side of the scale. The highly diluted "very bare knowledge" of the offended in these cases can hardly have very great weight.

Traditionally, liberals have categorically rejected statutes penalizing harmless unwitnessed private conduct no matter how profoundly upset *anyone* may become at the bare knowledge that such conduct is or might be occurring. Mill had deep and well-justified suspicions of the good faith of the parties who claim to need protection of their own sensibilities from the self-regarding conduct of others,[16] and he offered many examples of liberties unfairly withdrawn from minorities on the disingenuous ground that the prohibited conduct, even when harmless and unwitnessed, was a deep affront to the others: the liberty to eat pork (in Moslem countries), to worship God as a Protestant or Jew (in Spain), to perform music, dance, play games, or attend theatres on the Sabbath (in Puritan Great Britain and New England), to drink beer in one's own home (during Prohibition in the United States).

H. L. A. Hart is even more emphatic:

> The fundamental objection surely is that a right to be protected
> from the distress which is inseparable from the bare knowledge that

others are acting in ways you think wrong, cannot be acknowledged
by anyone who recognizes individual liberty as a value. For the . . .
principle that coercion may be used to protect [persons] . . . from
this form of distress cannot stop there. If distress incident to the
belief that others are doing wrong is harm [better "preventable
offense"], so also is the distress incident to the belief that others are
doing what you do not want them to do; and the only liberty that
could coexist with this extension of . . . the principle is liberty to do
those things to which no one seriously objects. Such liberty is clearly
nugatory.[17]

Hart overstates his case here somewhat. If the prohibition of
unwitnessed acts were limited to profound offenses, and balancing tests were scrupulously observed, there would be little danger
that the offense principle so mediated could commit legislatures
to banning private conduct by some parties on the ground that
other parties don't *want* them acting that way *simpliciter*. And
provided balancing tests are assumed, it is a *non sequitur* to say
that the only permitted liberty would be "the liberty to do those
things to which *no one* seriously objects;" rather the sole liberty
would be to do those things to which *not everybody* (or nearly
everybody) seriously objects. Nevertheless, Hart's point is a
sobering one that should take away the appetite of any liberal for
criminalizing harmless and unobserved behavior or any kind:

> Recognition of individual liberty as a value involves, as a mini-
> mum, acceptance of the principle that the individual may do as he
> wants, even if others are distressed when they learn what it is that
> he does—unless of course there are other good grounds for forbid-
> ding it. No social order which accords to individual liberty any
> value could also accord the right to be protected from distress thus
> occasioned.[18]

Again, there is some overstatement. One could hold that liberty
has *some* value and that prevention of distress at bare knowledge
has some value too, so that the two must sometimes be balanced
against one another. But Hart's point does seem to apply to the
view that defines the *liberal's* values (see Vol. 1, Introduction, §5),
namely that liberty has very great value indeed, and not simply "a

value" or "any value". It is impossible that liberty should at once have great value and be properly sacrificed to prevent "mere distress" to others caused by their bare or very bare knowledge. And even though the protection of moral sensibility from profound offense does not logically imply the protection of persons from *any* kind of distress, it is true as a matter of empirical fact (and this was Mill's major emphasis) that legislatures are prone to slide in that direction once they start down the slope.

The endorsement of the offense principle by the liberal theorist thus creates tensions for him in two directions. Those who are impressed with the unique character of profound offense urge a relaxing of the normal balancing tests derived from nuisance law for determining when offenses are serious enough to warrant criminal prohibition, so that even unwitnessed offensive conduct might be prohibited in some circumstances. Those who are impressed by the great value of liberty, on the other hand, urge the liberal theorist to stand more resolutely against any acceptance of criminal statutes that ban harmless and unwitnessed conduct. These liberals often argue that the balancing tests are not protection enough, since in some cases the tests might themselves warrant punishment of unobserved and harmless actions, so that they should be replaced by more categorical protection. My position up until this point in the book has been to resist the pressure to grant an exemption to "profound offense" from the requirements of the normal mediating standards for the application of the offense principle, while reassuring my fellow liberals that the balancing tests are not likely ever to permit offense at bare knowledge to outweigh any private and harmless offending conduct, and certainly not any that has the slightest hint of redeeming value. But perhaps I was too sanguine.

4. Solution of the Bare Knowledge Problem

My argument for the adequacy of the balancing tests rested on the assumption that secret and private activity is never the object of *serious* offense, because the offense it causes cannot be as intense or widespread as that caused by directly observed conduct, and such as it is, it is always "reasonably avoidable." Where there are exceptions to these generalizations, I assumed that they were the consequence of an excessive, even pathological, susceptibility to offense that can hardly warrant interference with any wholly self-regarding actions of others that are minimally reasonable, that is, either individually or socially valuable, discreet as can be expected without forfeiting the right of free expression, and not maliciously or spitefully *intended* to offend those who are excessively susceptible to offense. The key assumption, of course, is that only the excessively "skittish" would bolt at the mere idea of harmless but repugnant unobserved conduct, and *their* reactions, like that of rare skittish horses, cannot be the ground for interfering with otherwise innocent or valuable activity that cannot conveniently be done in a way to avoid upsetting the skittish.

The argument from moral skittishness, however, does not give the nervous liberal all the protection he needs, and no doubt both Mill and Hart would feel insecure with it. It is no doubt true, as a matter of fact, of the western democracies in the twentieth century that extreme, widespread, and inescapable offense at unobserved but disapproved harmless conduct is possible only for the morally skittish. But there is no necessity that this connection hold universally, for all societies in all ages. What if this kind of susceptibility to offense ceased to be rare and exceptional? What if it spread through the whole community and became a new norm of susceptibility? Then clearly it would no longer be, in the same sense, excessive or "skittish." We can ask the same questions about *literal* skittishness. What if 99% of all domestic horses, and hence the statistically "average" horse, came to have just the characteristics we have in mind *now* when we call a given horse "skittish"? We don't call the average horse skittish, because "skittish" means abnormally or exceptionally nervous, and the normal horse cannot, in the statistical sense, be abnormal. We would have to raise our standards of skittishness so that only those horses who were more nervous even than the new average would be properly called "skittish." It would still be true that people should not be liable for starting skittish horses through their otherwise routine and useful behavior, but people could rightly be required to be more careful than they are now in the way they act before the normal horses.

The analogy is plain. In Saudi Arabia, it may well be that 90% of the population is morally skittish by our standards even though "normal" of course by their own. In the United States almost everyone would be put into intensely disagreeable offended states by the repulsive conduct on the bus of Chapter 7, but hardly anyone would be put into equally disagreeable and unavoidable states by the bare idea of such conduct occurring at a known place in private, or simply occurring somewhere or other (for all one knows) because it is legal. But it is at least conceivable (barely) that almost all Saudis are put in precisely the same intensely unpleasant state of mind by the thought that wine or pork is being consumed somewhere or Christian rites conducted somewhere in their country beyond their perception as they would be by their direct witnessing of such odious conduct. For at least some of these examples, our balancing tests would pose no barrier to legitimate criminal prohibition. In particular, where the private conduct is neither expressive (because there is no audience with which to communicate) nor religious, and without other redeeming social importance or personal value (it consists, say, of the actual defacing and smashing of religious icons or patriotic emblems), then its value might not outbalance the inescapably intense offense suffered by all "normal" outsiders at the bare knowledge of what is going on. And so the liberal's argument concludes that although the balancing tests work well to render illegitimate the criminalization here and now of private harmless acts, they could be used, unfortunately, to legitimize criminal statutes in more homogeneous and authoritarian societies where minorities, actual and potential, are even more in need of protection.

It must be conceded in response, that the offense principle mediated by the balancing tests does not give the liberal all the reassurance he needs. That is not to say that it fails to give him any substantial reassurance, but only that it falls short of a guarantee against misapplication. It cannot be used in any society to punish, on grounds of offensiveness merely, acts of expression (to non-captive audiences) or of private religious rituals, or of voluntary sexual conduct in private (with its great personal value to the participants). But it can be used to protect persons from "profound offense" when it is almost equally unpleasant as the worst of the public nuisances, and is so to almost everyone, and the offending private conduct has little redeeming value. These are conditions not likely to be satisfied in our own society, but conceivably would be satisfied elsewhere. The liberal can be further reassured, however, that even where the offense principle legitimizes in principle a prohibition, it is not likely that a legislature would find justifying reasons on balance for enacting the legislation. Either the offending conduct would be so eccentric and infrequent that it would not be cost-efficient to bother with it, or else for other practical reasons enforcement would have unacceptable side effects. The statute itself would encourage busybodies, eavesdroppers, and informers, require police to engage in unsavory detection practices, or else put the privacy of everyone in jeopardy, lead to arbitrarily selective enforcement, increase the leverage of blackmailers, and, in general, use expensive police resources in unproductive or counterproductive ways. Finally, even if there were such prohibitive statutes, since they are based only on the offense principle, they could rightly impose only minor penalties (see Chap. 7, §1) and would therefore have little deterrent value. So the liberal need not fear that legislative acceptance of the offense principle would pose an immediate threat to our liberties here and now. But that is not strong enough assurance. What he needs is a way of demonstrating that punishment of wholly private and harmless conduct for the purpose of preventing offended reactions occasioned by the bare knowledge that such conduct is or could be occurring is *illegitimate in principle*, and thus always wrong, here or elsewhere. To reach that conclusion, a different and supplementary liberal strategy is needed.

Let me return to the concept of "profound offense". If governmental invasions of liberty to protect others from bare knowledge are *ever* legitimate, it must surely be when the resultant offense is of the "profound" variety. If mere offense to the senses or the lower-order sensibilities (e.g. by "disgusting" activities) could be protected even from unwitnessed conduct, then as we have seen,

the offendable party would be protected from conduct to which
he has no objection except that it is unpleasant to witness, and
then even when he is not made to witness it! In that case what he
is actually protected against is his own vivid imaginings, which
should be subject to his own control unless they are, because of
neurosis, irresistibly obsessive. In the case of genuinely profound
offenses, however, the offended party has a powerful objection to
the unwitnessed conduct quite apart from the effects on his own
state of mind that come from thinking about it when it is unobserved. Indeed, these derivative unpleasant effects are the consequence of the behavior's affront to his moral sensibilities and
would not exist but for that affront. It would put the cart before
the horse to say that the moral sensibilities are shocked because of
the unpleasant states produced in the offended party's mind.
These states have nothing to do with his complaint. His grievance is not a personal one made in his own behalf. It is therefore
odd to ground a prohibition of the offending conduct on a fancied
need to protect *him*.[19] When an unwitnessed person defaces flags
and mutilates corpses in the privacy of his own rooms, the out-
sider is outraged, but *he* would not claim to be the *victim* of the
offensive behavior. He thinks that the behavior is wrong whether
it has a true victim or not, and *that* is what outrages him. As soon
as he shifts his attention to his own discomfiture, the whole
nature of his complaint will change, and his moral fervor will seep
out like air through a punctured inner tube.

But if it is not the offended party himself who needs "protection" from unobserved harmless conduct, who can it possibly be
that can make claim to "protection"? Whose rights are violated
when an impersonal object is smashed in the privacy of the desce-
crator's rooms? Surely not the object itself; it is not the kind of
thing that can have rights in the first place. Surely not the dese-
crator. He is acting voluntarily and doing exactly what he wants.
Perhaps it is an evil that sacred symbols, artificial or natural,
should be defaced, whether observed or not. But it doesn't seem
to be the kind of evil that can be the basis of anyone's grievance.

The advocate of punishment for those whose unwitnessed and
unharmful activities offend in their very description can now be

confronted with a dilemma. Either he bases his argument on an application of the offense principle or else on a (tacit) appeal to the illiberal principle of legal moralism. The former would be a claim to protection from their own unpleasant mental states by those who are offended by a "bare thought" or by "bare knowledge" of the occurrence of the loathsome behavior. The latter would be an application of the liberty-limiting principle that all liberals (by definition) reject: that it is a good reason for a criminal prohibition that it is necessary to prevent inherently immoral conduct whether or not that conduct causes harm or offense to anyone. If it is the liberal offense principle to which ultimate appeal is made, the argument has a fatal flaw. According to that principle as we have interpreted it (Chap. 7, §1) criminal law may be used to protect persons from *wrongful offense*, that is, from their own unpleasant mental states when wrongfully imposed on them by other parties in a manner that violates their rights. On the plausible assumption that desecration of sacred symbols even in private is wrong (even without a victim), there is a sense then in which it produces "wrongful offense" in the mind of any disapproving person who learns about it: The conduct is wrongful *and* it is a cause of a severely offended mental state. But that is not yet sufficient for it to be a "wrongful offense" in the sense intended in a truly liberal offense principle. The offense-causing action must be more than wrong; it must be *a wrong* to the offended party, in short a violation of *his* rights.[20] But as we have seen, even the offended party himself will not claim that his own rights have been necessarily violated by any unobserved conduct that he thinks of as morally odious. If he does make that further personal claim he becomes vulnerable to Mill's withering charges of moral egotism and bad faith. (See notes 12, 13, and 16 *supra*.) His profoundly offended condition then is not a wrong to him, and thus not a "wrongful offense" in the sense of the liberal offense principle.

The offended party experiences moral shock, revulsion, and indignation, not on his own behalf of course, but on behalf of his moral principles or his moral regard for precious symbols. If those moral reactions are to be the ground for legal coercion and punishment of the offending conduct, it must be by virtue of the principle of legal moralism which enforces moral conviction and gives effect to moral outrage even when there are no violated rights, and in general no persons to "protect". The liberal, however, is adamantly opposed to the principle of legal moralism, and he sees no reason to let into the criminal law on offense-principle grounds what he insists on excluding when candidly presented on moralistic grounds. In summary, the argument for criminalization of private conduct to prevent bare-knowledge offense rests either on the offense principle or on legal moralism. If it appeals to the liberal's offense principle it fails, since bare-knowledge offense is not "wrongful offense" in the sense employed by that principle. But if it appeals to legal moralism, it may be valid on those grounds, but it cannot commit the liberal, since the liberal rejects legal moralism. It follows that there is no argument open to a liberal that legitimizes punishment of private harmless behavior in order to prevent bare-knowledge offense. Moreover, the liberal can continue to endorse the offense principle without fear of embarrassment. John Stuart Mill can rest secure.

There is, however, a complication to add of this solution to the bare-knowledge problem. There may be some cases of unwitnessed bare-knowledge offense where the case for banning the conduct that causes it does not require legal moralism. I refer to those *personal* deep affronts, whose victims claim that a personal grievance remains even after the moralistic case is severed from their argument. That is because the offending conduct is somehow addressed to them in an unmistakably direct way, even when not observed by them. For example, it should be illegal to acquire a corpse and conduct violent accident research on it (see *infra*, §5) without the next of kin's consent. If that were not so, a widow, for example, might learn that her dear late husband's face is being smashed to bits in a scientific experiment, whether she likes it or not. She does not have to witness it (fortunately) but she suffers at the bare thought, which she cannot keep out of her mind. Even when she is thinking of other things she is generally depressed. She has a grievance in this case that she does not share with every stranger who may know of the experiments and conscientiously disapprove of them. Her grievance is personal (voiced on her own behalf) not simply because her moral sensibility is affronted (she has no personal *right* not to have her moral sensibility affronted) and she cannot keep *that* out of her mind, but rather because it is *her* husband, and not someone else. In this quite exceptional kind of case, the personally related party is the only one whose rights are violated, though many others may suffer profound offense at the bare knowledge. (Racist mockery and abusive pornography received "in private" by willing audiences can also cause acutely *personal* offense to members of the insulted groups who have bare knowledge of it, and must therefore be treated as exceptional cases. See the discussions below in §§7 and 8, especially in chapter 11, §9.) Her rights therefore would be more economically protected by injunctive orders or civil actions than by the criminal law.

One hard question remains. What of the bare-knowledge offender (say a human flesh-eater who receives his dead bodies through donations or other legal means) who engages in his profoundly offensive activity in private, and who not only makes no effort to conceal the fact, but "openly and notoriously" flaunts his tastes, invites others to join in his activities, openly advertises for others to join him, even with garish neon signs (as in Kurt Baier's example)? Those to whom the human body is a sacred icon are not only morally shocked at the very idea of cannibalism; they are prevented by the advertisement from ridding their minds of the shocking idea whose offensiveness is revitalized by every encounter with the intrusive sign. I think the liberal principles can warrant interference with excessive displays of this character, though not with the basic rights of privacy, communication, and expression. But the balance of conflicting values is delicate, and the risk of erroneous judgment great.

Consider a spectrum of cases. In the first, the lonely cannibal solicits collaborators by phone calls to his friends, letters, and private conversation only. If it is his right to engage in the primary offensive behavior in private (and in the absence of harm to others, the liberal cannot deny that right), then surely it is his right to talk about it with others and invite them to join him. If he solicits strangers on the street, however, and does so aggressively and tenaciously, he becomes a public nuisance, even a harasser. (See Chap.

16, §2.) Suppose now a second example, in which discreet and dignified advertisements are placed on his building, and notices put in newspapers. Still the liberal has no objection. The third example is our original one, in which the advertisement is by means of a garish neon sign. In the fourth example, the advertisements are on large billboards throughout the city and on huge neon signs on an elevated platform dominating the downtown center of the city. Finally, in the fifth example, the conspicuous signs are now illustrated graphically with paintings (say) of attractive men and women carving rump roasts out of a recognizably human corpse.

The liberal could approve banning the graphic signs on ordinary nuisance grounds. The public streets are for many as inescapable as the public bus was for the unfortunate passengers in Chapter 7, and vivid depictions of conduct can be as disgusting, nauseating, grating, embarrassing, or irritating as the actual behavior depicted. The fourth example is more difficult. If the conspicuous and unavoidable non-graphic signs are to be prohibited, it must be because they alter the public environment in a way that misrepresents the public intention. Every part of a city might belong to someone or other, but the city as a whole represents all its citizens. They might wish to have trees planted along all the public thoroughfares, or build monuments to public heroes, or decorate public spaces with sculpture, works of art, and plaques with lines of classic poetry. Even the great dominating neon signs illuminating the night on Broadway or Piccadilly Circus, though they are on private land and communicate private messages to the public, create a unique city ambience that becomes a kind of distinctive public possession and a symbol of the city to outsiders. When the more visible "monuments" include invitations to cannibalism, sodomy, symbol desecration, flag burning, and corpse mutilating, among other harmless eccentricities, then the public ambience of the city has been quite unsubtly altered, to the detriment of a public interest. "Is this really what we want the symbol of our city to be?", the citizens might ask, and provided less destructive modes of communication and advertisement are left open, the liberal might not object if the citizens answer "No!", and take appropriate regulative action.

The example with which we began, the single neon sign, is a borderline case, just because it is an isolated instance and not likely to affect the visual environment of the city as a whole. It could offend, however, as a kind of eyesore, indeed even as a neon sign advertising beer, or church worship, or philosophy books, might be an eyesore in some neighborhoods. But even its written message itself, being an affront to what is held by many to be sacred, when aggressively obtruded upon the attention of passersby, is a kind of public nuisance. It is not an illiberal response to say: "I don't care what you do in private; that is your business. But stop making me a party to it, by rubbing my nose in it." The private unobserved eating of human flesh is like the private unobserved desecrating of a holy symbol. The neon sign advertising it, on the other hand, is like the *public* desecrating of a holy symbol, like displaying on one's house an illuminated cross defaced with obscene figures and messages to scandalize the pious. There is a sense in which desecration cannot truly *be* desecration unless it is public. When it is public, and more than is necessary for some legitimate purpose, it crosses the line of offensive nuisance. Words, of course, are not the same as pictures, and pictures are not the same as real conduct right out in public. Perhaps then "desecration" is too strong a word for mere words that call attention to desecration, itself unobserved. The lonely cannibal could receive the benefit of that doubt if he ceased using garish neon, and advertised less aggressively.

Notes

*Editor's note: References to chapters 7 and 8, here and throughout this essay, refer to chapters in Feinberg's book *Offense to Other,* volume 2 of *The Moral Limits of the Criminal Law* (New York: Oxford University Press, 1985).

1. Robert Paul Wolff, *The Poverty of Liberalism* (Boston: Beacon Press, 1968), p. 24.

2. Louis B. Schwartz, "Morals Offenses and the Model Penal Code," *Columbia Law Review* 63 (1963), as reprinted in Joel Feinberg and Hyman Gross, eds., *Philosophy of Law,* 2d ed. (Belmont, Calif.: Wadsworth Publishing Co., 1980), p. 215, n. 14.

3. Pa. Stat. Ann. tit. 18, §4211 (1945).

4. Schwartz, *op. cit.* (footnote 2), 210.

5. *Loc. cit.*

6. *Ibid.,* p. 211.

7. *Loc. cit.*

8. For fuller lists of suggested "person-making characteristics," and fuller discussion, see Joseph Fletcher, "Indicators of Humanhood: A Tentative Profile of Man," *Hastings Center Report*, Vol. 2 (1972), Laurence C. Becker, "Human Being: The Boundaries of the Concept," *Philosophy and Public Affairs*. Vol. 4 (1975), Mary Anne Warren, "On the Moral and Legal Status of Abortion," and Michael Tooley, "In Defense of Abortion and Infanticide." The Warren and Tooley articles are both included in *The Problem of Abortion*, 2d ed., ed. Joel Feinberg (Belmont, Calif.: Wadsworth Publishing Co., 1983).

9. Kurt Baier, "The Liberal to Pornography," *University of Pittsburgh Law Review* 40 (1979), p. 620.

10. Baier, *op. cit.*, p. 621, spells out a corollary to this point.

Disgusting behavior *offends* the senses of those who encounter it because it disgusts them. In such cases, what offends is what disgusts, i.e. the direct physical onslaught on the senses. Disgust, offense to a person, and so a [true] offense, can be avoided by preventing such onslaught. If I love the smell of burnt rubber, I can avoid offending and becoming guilty of an offense by making sure that the smell does not escape and bother my neighbors. I do not offend them by boasting of my unusual predilections or inviting them to sniffing parties. There is no standard of propriety violated by my indulging my taste.

11. For an example of a similar odd conviction, see Bertrand Russell, *Unpopular Essays* (New York: Simon and Schuster, 1950), pp. 75–76.

I am sometimes shocked by the blasphemies of those who think themselves pious—for instance the nuns who never take a bath without wearing a bathrobe all the time. When asked why, since no man can see them, they reply: "Oh, but you forget the good God." Apparently they conceive of the Deity as a Peeping Tom whose omnipotence enables Him to see through bathroom walls, but who is foiled by bathrobes. This view strikes me as curious.

12. John Stuart Mill, *On Liberty*, chap. 4, para. 12.

13. *Loc. cit.*

14. Kurt Baier, *op. cit.* (footnote 8), pp. 621–22.

15. Louis Schwartz, *op. cit.* (footnote 2), p. 210.

16. J. S. Mill, *op. cit.* (footnote 11). In chap. 4, para. 12, Mill writes:

. . . the opinion of a majority, imposed as a law on the minority, on questions of self-regarding conduct is quite as likely to be wrong as right, for in these cases public opinion means, at the best, some people's opinion of what is good or bad for other people, while very often it does not even mean that—the public with the most perfect indifference, passing over the pleasure or convenience of those whose conduct they censure and considering only their own preference. There are many who consider as an injury to themselves any conduct which they have a distaste for, and resent it as an outrage to their feelings . . . when does a public trouble itself about universal experience? In its interferences with personal conduct it is seldom thinking of anything but the enormity of acting or feeling differently from itself . . .

17. H. L. A. Hart, *Law, Liberty, and Morality* (Stanford, Calif.: Stanford University Press, 1963), pp. 46–47.

18. *Ibid.*, p. 47.

19. The antiabortionist whose human sentiments are outraged at the thought of surgical mutilation and destruction of recognizably human "unborn babies," for exam-

ple, does not express indignation at what is done thereby to his *own* peace of mind. That is precisely why he is not placated by the principle "out of sight out of mind." His offended state of mind, therefore, is more typical of profound offense than of mere aversion to gross, irritating, or embarrassing sights. That is why we should say that his moral sensibility and not merely his delicacy is affronted.

20. In this respect too the offense principle is parallel to the harm principle. Just as the harm principle legitimizes coercion meant to prevent all those harms that are also wrongs to their victims, so the offense principle legitimizes prevention of all those offenses that are also wrongs to *their* victims. Both principles (and therefore all liberal liberty-limiting principles) are right-protecting principles.

8

The Doctrine of Liberty in Its
Application to Morals

James Fitzjames Stephen

These explanations enable me to restate without fear of misapprehension the object of morally intolerant legislation. It is to establish, to maintain, and to give power to that which the legislator regards as a good moral system or standard. For the reasons already assigned I think that this object is good if and in so far as the system so established and maintained is good. How far any particular system is good or not is a question which probably does not admit of any peremptory final decision; but I may observe that there are a considerable number of things which appear good and bad, though on doubt in different degrees, to all mankind. For the practical purpose of legislation refinements are of little importance. In any given age and nation virtue and vice have meanings which for that purpose are quite definite enough. In England at the present day many theories about morality are current, and speculative men differ about them widely, but they relate not so much to the question whether particular acts are right or wrong, as to the question of the precise meaning of the distinction, the manner in which the moral character of particular actions is to be decided, and the reasons for preferring right to wrong conduct. The result is that the object of promoting virtue and preventing vice must be admitted to be both a good one and one sufficiently intelligible for legislative purposes.

If this is so, the only remaining questions will be as to the efficiency of the means at the disposal of society for this purpose, and the cost of their application. Society has at its disposal two great instruments by which vice may be prevented and virtue promoted—namely, law and public opinion; and law is either criminal or civil. The use of each of these instruments is subject to certain limits and conditions, and the wisdom of attempting to make men good either by Act of Parliament or by the action of public opinion depends entirely upon the degree in which those limits and conditions are recognized and acted upon.

First, I will take the case of criminal law. What are the conditions under which and the limitations within which it can be applied with success to the object of making men better? In considering this question it must be borne in mind that criminal law is at once by far the most powerful and by far the roughest engine which society can use for any purpose. Its power is shown by the fact that it can and does render crime exceedingly difficult and dangerous. Indeed, in civilized society it absolutely prevents avowed open crime committed with the strong hand, except in cases where crime rises to the magnitude of civil war. Its roughness hardly needs illustration. It strikes so hard that it can be enforced only on the gravest occasions, and with every sort of precaution against abuse or mistake. Before an act can be treated as a crime, it ought to be capable of distinct definition and of specific proof, and it ought also to be of such a nature that it is worth while to prevent it at the risk of inflicting great damage, direct and indirect, upon those who commit it. These conditions are seldom, if ever, fulfilled by mere vices. It would obviously be impossible to indict a man for ingratitude or perfidy. Such charges are too vague for specific discussion and distinct proof on the one side, and disproof on the other. Moreover, the expense of the investigations necessary for the legal punishment of such conduct would be enormous. It would be necessary to go into an infinite number of delicate and subtle inquiries which would tear off all privacy from the lives of a large number of persons. These considerations are, I think, conclusive reasons against treating vice in general as a crime.

The excessive harshness of criminal law is also a circumstance which very greatly narrows the range of its application. It is the *ratio ultima* of the majority against persons whom its application assumes to have renounced the common bonds which connect men together. When a man is subjected to legal punishment, society appeals directly and exclusively to his fears. It renounces the attempt to work upon his affections or feelings. In other words, it puts itself into distinct, harsh, and undisguised opposition to his wishes; and the effect of this will be to make him rebel against the law. The violence of the rebellion will be measured partly by the violence of the passion the indulgence of which is forbidden, and partly by the degree to which the law can count upon an ally in the man's own conscience. A law which enters into a direct contest with a fierce imperious passion, which the person who feels it does not admit to be bad, and which is not directly injurious to others, will generally do more harm than good; and this is perhaps the principal reason why it is impossible to legislate directly against unchastity, unless it takes forms which every one regards as monstrous and horrible. The subject is not one for detailed discussion, but any one who will follow out the reflections which this hint suggests will find that they supply a striking illustration of the limits which the harshness of criminal law imposes upon its range.

If we now look at the different acts which satisfy the conditions specified, it will, I think, be found that criminal law in this country actually is applied to the suppression of vice and so to the promotion of virtue to a very considerable extent; and this I say is right.

The punishment of common crimes, the gross forms of force and fraud, is no doubt ambiguous. It may be justified on the principle of self-protection, and apart from any question as to their moral character. It is not, however, difficult to show that these acts have in fact been forbidden and subjected to punishment not only because they are dangerous to society, and so ought to be prevented, but also for the sake of gratifying the feeling of hatred—call it revenge, resentment, or what you will—which the contemplation of such conduct excites in healthily constituted minds. If this can be shown, it will follow that criminal law is in the nature of a persecution of the grosser forms of vice, and an emphatic assertion of the principle that the feeling of hatred and the desire of vengeance above-mentioned are important elements of human nature which ought in such cases to be satisfied in a regular public and legal manner.

The strongest of all proofs of this is to be found in the principles universally admitted and acted upon as regulating the amount of punishment. If vengeance affects, and ought to affect, the amount of punishment, every circumstance which aggravates or extenuates the wickedness of an act will operate in aggravation or diminution of punishment. If the object of legal punishment is simply the prevention of specific acts, this will not be the case. Circumstances which extenuate the wickedness of the crime will often operate in aggravation of punishment. If, as I maintain, both objects must be kept in view, such circumstances will operate in different ways according to the nature of the case.

A judge has before him two criminals, one of whom appears, from the circumstances of the case, to be ignorant and depraved, and to have given way to very strong temptation, under the influence of the other, who is a man of rank and education, and who committed the offence of which both are convicted under comparatively slight temptation. I will venture to say that if he made any difference between them at all every judge on the English bench would give the first man a lighter sentence than the second.

What should we think of such an address to the prisoners as this? You, A, are a most dangerous man. You are ignorant, you are depraved, and you are accordingly peculiarly liable to be led into crime by the solicitations or influence of people like your accomplice B. Such influences constitute to men like you a temptation practically all but irresistible. The class to which you belong is a large one, and is accessible only to the coarsest possible motives. For these reasons I must put into the opposite scale as heavy a weight as I can, and the sentence of the court upon you is that you be taken to the place from whence you came and from thence to a place of execution, and that there you be hanged by the neck till you are dead. As to you, B, you are undoubtedly an infamous wretch. Between you and your tool A there can, morally speaking, be no comparison at all. But I have nothing to do with that. You belong to a small and not a dangerous class. The temptation to which you gave way was slight, and the impression made upon me by your conduct is that you really did not care very much whether you committed this crime or not. From a moral point of view, this may perhaps increase your guilt; but it shows that the motive to be overcome is less powerful in your case than in A's. You belong, moreover, to a class, and occupy a position in society, in which exposure and loss of character are much dreaded. This you will have to undergo. Your case is a very odd one, and it is not likely that you will wish to commit such a crime again, or that others will follow your example. Upon the whole, I think that what has passed will deter others from such conduct as much as actual punishment. It is, however, necessary to keep a hold over you. You will therefore be discharged on your own recognizance to come up and receive judgment when called upon, and unless you conduct yourself better for the future, you will assuredly be so called upon, and if you do not appear, your recognizance will be inexorably forfeited.

Caricature apart, the logic of such a view is surely unimpeachable. If all that you want of criminal law is the prevention of crime by the direct fear of punishment, the fact that a temptation is strong is a reason why punishment should be severe. In some instances this actually is the case. It shows the reason why political crimes and offences against military discipline are punished so severely. But in most cases the strength of the temptation operates in mitigation of punishment, and the reason of this is that criminal law operates not merely by producing fear, but also indirectly, but very powerfully, by giving distinct shape to the feeling of anger, and a distinct satisfaction to the desire of vengeance which crime excites in a healthy mind.

Other illustrations of the fact that English criminal law does recognize morality are to be found in the fact that a considerable number of acts which need not be specified are treated as crimes merely because they are regarded as grossly immoral.

I have already shown in what manner Mr. Mill deals with these topics. It is, I venture to think, utterly unsatisfactory. The impression it makes upon me is that he feels that such acts ought to be punished, and that he is able to reconcile this with his fundamental principles only by subtleties quite unworthy of him. Admit the relation for which I am contending between law and morals, and all becomes perfectly clear. All the acts referred to are unquestionably wicked. Those who do them are ashamed of them. They are all capable of being clearly defined and specifically proved or disproved, and there can be no question at all that legal punishment reduces them to small dimensions, and forces the criminals to carry on their practices with secrecy and precaution. In other words, the object of their suppression is good, and the means adequate. In practice this is subject to highly important qualifications, of which I will only say here that those who have due regard to the incurable weaknesses of human nature will be very careful how they inflict penalties upon mere vice, or even upon those who make a trade of promoting it, unless special circumstances call for their infliction. It is one thing however to tolerate vice so long as it is inoffensive, and quite another to give it a legal right not only to exist, but to assert itself in the face of the world as an 'experiment in living' as good as another, and entitled to the same protection from law.

I now pass to the manner in which civil law may and does, and as I say properly, promote virtue and prevent vice. This is a subject so wide that I prefer indicating its nature by a few illustrations to attempting to deal with it systematically. It would, however, be easy to show that nearly every branch of civil law assumes the existence of a standard of moral good and evil which the public at large have an interest in maintaining, and in many cases enforcing—a proceeding which is diametrically opposed to Mr. Mill's fundamental principles.[1]

The main subject with which law is conversant is that of rights and duties, and all the commoner and more important rights and duties presuppose some theory of morals. Contracts are one great source of rights and duties. Is there any country in the world the courts of which would enforce a contract which the Legislature regarded as immoral? and is there any country in which there would be much difficulty in specific cases in saying whether the object or the consideration of a contract was or was not immoral? Other rights are of a more general nature, and are liable to be violated by wrongs. Take the case of a man's right to his reputation, which is violated by defamation. How, without the aid of some sort of theory of morals, can it be determined whether the publication of defamatory matter is justifiable or not?

Perhaps the most pointed of all illustrations of the moral character of civil law is to be found in the laws relating to marriage and inheritance. They all proceed upon an essentially moral theory as to the relation of the sexes. Take the case of illegitimate children. A bastard is *filius nullius*—he inherits nothing, he has no claim on his putative father. What is all this except the expression of the strongest possible determination on the part of the Legislature to recognize, maintain, and favour marriage in every possible manner as the foundation of civilized society? It has been plausibly maintained that these laws bear hardly upon bastards, punishing them for the sins of their parents. It is not necessary to my purpose to go into this, though it appears to me that the law is right. I make the remark merely for the sake of showing to what lengths the law does habitually go for the purpose of maintaining the most important of all moral principles, the principle upon which one great department of it is entirely founded. It is a case in which a good object is promoted by efficient and adequate means.

These illustrations are so strong that I will add nothing more to them from this branch of the law, but I may refer to a few miscellaneous topics which bear on the same subject. Let us take first the case of sumptuary laws. Mr. Mill's principles would no doubt condemn them, and, as they have gone out of fashion, it may be said, that unless my principle does so too, it is the worse for my principle. I certainly should not condemn sumptuary laws on the principle that the object in view is either bad or improper for legislation. I can hardly imagine a greater blessing to the whole community than a reduction in the lavish extravagance which makes life so difficult and laborious. It is difficult for me to look at a lace machine with patience. The ingenuity which went to devise it might have made human life materially happier in a thousand ways, and its actual effect has been to enable a great number of people to wear an imitation of an ornament which derives what little merit it has principally from its being made by hand. If any one could practically solve the problem of securing the devotion of the higher forms of human ingenuity to objects worthy of them, he would be an immense benefactor to his species. Life, however, has become so complicated, vested interests are so powerful and so worthy of respect, it is so clear that the enforcement of any conceivable law upon such a subject would be impossible, that I do not think anyone in these days would be found to propose one. In a simpler age of the world and in a smaller community such laws may have been very useful. The same remarks apply to laws as to the distribution of property and to the regulation of trade.

Laws relating to education and to military service and the discipline of the army have a moral side of the utmost importance. Mr. Mill would be the first to admit this; indeed, in several passages of his book he insists on the fact that society has complete control over the rising generation as a reason why it should not coerce adults into morality. This surely is the very opposite of the true conclusion. How is it possible for society to accept the position of an educator unless it has moral principles on which to educate? How, having accepted that position and having educated people up to a certain point, can it draw a line at which education ends and perfect moral indifference begins? When a private man educates his family, his superiority over them is founded principally on his superior age and experience; and as this personal superiority ceases, the power which is founded upon it gradually ceases also. Between society at large and individuals the difference is of another kind. The fixed principles and institutions of society express not merely the present opinions of the ruling part of the community, but the accumulated results of centuries of experience, and these constitute a standard by which the conduct of individuals may be tried, and to which they are in a variety of ways, direct and indirect, compelled to conform. This, I think, is one of the meanings which may be attached to the assertion that education never ceases. As a child grows into a man, and as a young man grows into an old man, he is brought under the influence of successive sets of educators, each of whom sets its mark upon him. It is no uncommon thing to see aged parents taught by their grown-up children lessons learned by the children in their intercourse with their own generation. All of us are continually educating each other, and in every instance this is and must be a process at once moral and more or less coercive.[2]

As to Mr. Mill's doctrine that the coercive influence of public opinion ought to be exercised only for self-protective purposes, it seems to me a paradox so startling that it is almost impossible to argue against it. A single consideration on the subject is sufficient to prove this. The principle is one which it is impossible to carry out. It is like telling a rose that it ought to smell sweet only for the purpose of affording pleasure to the owner of the ground in which it grows. People form and express their opinions on each other, which, collectively, form public opinion, for a thousand reasons; to amuse themselves; for the sake of something to talk about; to gratify this or that momentary feeling; but the effect of such opinions, when formed, is quite independent of the grounds on their formation. A man is tried for murder, and just escapes conviction. People read the trial from curiosity; they discuss it for the sake of discussion; but if, by whatever means, they are brought to think that the man was in all probability guilty, they shun his society as they would shun any other hateful thing. The opinion produces its effect in precisely the same way whatever was its origin.

The result of these observations is that both law and public opinion do in many cases exercise a powerful coercive influence on morals, for objects which are good in the sense explained above, and by means well calculated to attain those objects, to a greater or less extent at a not inadequate expense. If this is so, I say law and public opinion do well, and I do not see how either the premises or the conclusion are to be disproved.

Of course there are limits to the possibility of useful interference with morals, either by law or by public opinion; and it is of the highest practical importance that these limits should be carefully observed. The great leading principles on the subject are few and simple, though they cannot be stated with any great precision. It will be enough to mention the following:

(1) Neither legislation nor public opinion ought to be meddlesome. A very large proportion of the matters upon which people wish to interfere with their neighbors are trumpery little things which are of no real importance at all. The busybody and world-betterer who will never let things alone, or trust people to take care of themselves, is a common and a contemptible character. The commonplaces directed against these small creatures are perfectly just, but to try to put them down by denying the connection between law and morals is like shutting all light and air out of a house in order to keep out gnats and blue-bottle flies.

(2) Both legislation and public opinion, but especially the latter, are apt to be most mischievous and cruelly unjust if they proceed upon imperfect evidence. To form and express strong opinions about the wickedness of a man whom you do not know, the immorality or impiety of a book you have not read, the merits of a question on which you are uninformed, is to run a great risk of inflicting a great wrong. It is hanging first and trying afterwards, or more frequently not trying at all. This, however, is no argument against hanging after a fair trial.

(3) Legislation ought in all cases to be graduated to the existing level of morals in the time and country in which it is employed. You cannot punish anything which public opinion, as expressed in the common practice of society, does not strenuously and unequivocally condemn. To try to do so is a sure way to produce gross hypocrisy and furious reaction. To be able to punish, a moral majority must be overwhelming. Law cannot be better than the nation in which it exists, though it may and can protect an acknowledged moral standard, and may gradually be increased in strictness as the standard rises. We punish, with the utmost severity, practices which in Greece and Rome went almost uncensured. It is possible that a time may come when it may appear natural and right to punish adultery, seduction, or possibly even fornication, but the prospect is, at present, indefinitely remote, and it may be doubted whether we are moving in that direction.

(4) Legislation and public opinion ought in all cases whatever scrupulously to respect privacy. To define the province of privacy distinctly is impossible, but it can be described in general terms. All the more intimate and delicate relations of life are of such a nature that to submit them to unsympathetic observation, or to observation which is sympathetic in the wrong way, inflicts great pain, and may inflict lasting moral injury. Privacy may be violated not only by the intrusion of a stranger, but by compelling or persuading a person to direct too much attention to his own feelings and to attach too much importance to their analysis. The common usage of language affords a practical test which is almost perfect upon this subject. Conduct which can be described as indecent is always in one way or another a violation of privacy. . . .

These, I think, are the principal forms in which society can and actually does promote virtue and restrain vice. It is impossible to form any estimate of the degree in which it succeeds in doing so, but it may perhaps be said that the principal importance of what is done in this direction by criminal law is that in extreme cases it brands gross acts of vice with the deepest mark of infamy which can be impressed upon them, and that in this manner it protects the public and accepted standard of morals from being grossly and openly violated. In short, it affirms in a singularly emphatic manner a principle which is absolutely inconsistent with and contradictory to Mr. Mill's—the principle, namely, that there are acts of wickedness so gross and outrageous that, self-protection apart, they must be prevented as far as possible at any cost to the offender, and punished, if they occur, with exemplary severity. . . .

Notes

1. Mr. Morley says on this: 'A good deal of rather bustling ponderosity is devoted to proving that the actual laws do in many points assume the existence of a standard of moral good and evil, and that this proceeding is diametrically opposed to Mr. Mill's fundamental principles. To this one would say first that the actual existence of laws of any given kind is wholly irrelevant to Mr. Mill's contention, which is that it would be better if laws of such a kind did not exist. Secondly, Mr. Mill never says, nor is it at all essential to his doctrine to hold, that a government ought not to have "a standard of

moral good and evil which the public at large have an interest in maintaining, and in many instances enforcing." He only set apart a certain class of cases to which the right or duty of enforcement of the criminal standard does not extend—self-regarding cases.'

As to the first point, surely it is not irrelevant to show that Mr. Mill is at issue with the practical conclusions to which most nations have been led by experience. Those to whom I address myself may be disposed to doubt whether a principle which condemns so many of the institutions under which they live can be right.

As to the second point, Mr. Mill says in express words: 'Society, as society, has no right to decide anything to be wrong which concerns only the individual.' This I think is equivalent to denying that society ought to have a moral standard, for by a moral standard I understand a judgment that certain acts are wrong, whoever they concern. Whether they concern the agent only or others as well, is and must be an accident. Mr. Morley, however, thinks that Mr. Mill's opinion was that society may and ought to have a moral standard, but ought not to enforce it in the case of self-regarding acts. I say, and attempt throughout the whole of this chapter to prove, that as regards the 'moral coercion of public opinion' this is neither possible nor desirable, and that as regards legal coercion, the question whether it is possible and desirable depends upon considerations drawn from the nature of law, civil and criminal. Whether I am right or wrong I cannot see that I have not understood Mr. Mill, or that I have not contradicted him.

2. Mr. Morley says in reference to this passage and the preceding passages from pp. [29–30]: 'Mr. Stephen . . . proves the contradictory of assertions which his adversary never made, as when he cites judicial instances which imply the recognition of morality by the law.' I think Mr. Morley misunderstands my argument, which nevertheless appears to me very plain. It is simply this: I say laws can and do promote virtue and diminish vice by coercion in the cases and in the ways specified, and their interference does more good than harm. The contradictory of this proposition would be that in the cases specified legal interference does more harm than good. Surely if Mr. Mill's general principle is true, this must follow from it. Therefore in denying it I deny a necessary inference from the principle which I attack.

Selected Bibliography

Berger, Fred. *Happiness, Justice and Freedom: The Moral and Political Philosophy of John Stuart Mill*. University of California Press, 1984. The best recent discussion of the whole of Mill's political philosophy.

Gray, John. *Mill on Liberty: A Defense*. Routledge, 1996. The most recent comprehensive discussion of Mill and liberty.

Himmelfarb, Gertrude. *On Liberty and Liberalism, The Case of John Stuart Mill*. Knopf, 1974. Discussion of Mill from a conservative point of view.

Radcliff, Peter ed. *Limits of Liberty: Studies of Mill's on Liberty*. Wadsworth, 1966. Somewhat dated but still useful set of critical commentaries.

Skorupski, John. *John Stuart Mill*. Routledge, 1989. A fair and thorough discussion of the whole of Mill's philosophy.

Stephen, James Fitzjames. *Liberty, Equality, Fraternity*. Liberty Press, 1993. A criticism of Mill by a contemporary. Still one of the most cogent.

Ten, C. L. *Mill on Liberty*. Oxford, 1980. A very comprehensive discussion of Mill and liberty.

Index

References followed by "n" or "nn" indicate notes.

About the Authors

David Lewis is professor of philosophy at Princeton University.

David Dyzenhaus is professor of law at the University of Toronto.

Robert Skipper is professor of philosophy at Southwest Texas State University.

Gerald Dworkin is professor of philosophy at the University of California, Davis, and the University of Illinois at Chicago.

Richard J. Arneson is professor of philosophy at the University of California, San Diego.

David Lyons is professor of law at Boston University.

Joel Feinberg is professor of philosophy at the University of Arizona.

James Fitzjames Stephen was a nineteenth-century British judge and historian of criminal law.